In the

— OF MY —

INHERITANCE

In the Shadow

—OF MY—

INHERITANCE

An Encouragement for Christlike Living

Michelle (Alias, The Kid")

May you determine to
cast a shadow of Christlikeness
to those you influence!

Love,
Jeanie
Ps. 37:4

JEANIE STEWART

REDEMPTION
PRESS

Published by Redemption Press, PO Box 427, Enumclaw, WA 98022.
Toll-Free (844) 2REDEEM (273-3336)

Redemption Press is honored to present this title in partnership with the author. The views expressed or implied in this work are those of the author. Redemption Press provides our imprint seal representing design excellence, creative content, and high-quality production.

The author has tried to recreate events, locales, and conversations from memories of them. In order to maintain their anonymity, in some instances the names of individuals, some identifying characteristics, and some details may have been changed, such as physical properties, occupations, and places of residence.

Unless otherwise indicated, all Scripture quotations are from the King James Version, public domain.

Scripture quotations marked (ESV) are from The ESV® Bible (The Holy Bible, English Standard Version®), copyright © 2001 by Crossway, a publishing ministry of Good News Publishers. Used by permission. All rights reserved.

ISBN 13: 978-1-64645-766-3 (Paperback)
978-1-64645-768-7 (ePub)
978-1-64645-767-0 (Mobi)

Library of Congress Catalog Card Number: 2022917403

Contents

Part II: Christlikeness: The Inheritance That Is Ours to Give

INTRODUCTION

WHEN I WAS FOUR YEARS OLD, I DISCOVERED MY OWN SHADOW. I was amazed that this alter ego moved wherever I did. Once I was no longer afraid of this new find, the game of chasing it would occupy me for quite some time.

One day a massive shadow overtook my small shadow, and I was even more amazed. At first I tried to escape the "monster" that overwhelmed my new "playmate," but once I discovered that the shadow was my father's, I delighted in standing in it. At six three, my dad cast a giant shadow for a child of four.

A shadow casts an image larger than itself—a phenomenon resulting from a brilliant light. Yet the image is familiar, for it is a silhouette of the person highlighted.

An inheritance is typically considered to be the stuff of wealth and property, but to me it is the character, beliefs, and influences passed on to us from our elder family members. Once those members have died, their legacy remains with us as shadows—their images existing only in our memories or in fading photographs. The most vibrant memories are the things that have impacted our lives the most, leading us to laugh, cry, learn, stand, or make major decisions.

Such is the inheritance in which I stand—an inheritance of faithful followers of Christ who, in numerous ways, have cast their shadows upon me, and I delight in them.

I make no apologies for the fact that I am a conservative-thinking, Bible-believing, God-called teacher of fifty years. I bring to this book no great credentials, no universally recognized name, and certainly no massive following. I bring only two things: vast years of life experience and, most gratefully, a godly heritage born from salvation in Christ Jesus. Those two things cause me to ponder the state of Christianity today.

I wonder what has gone wrong. Why are we seeming to lose the battle? Why are our children not following our leadership? Why are so many embracing secular humanism by departing the faith for a newfound faith in themselves? What liberal thinking has led to this calamity in the body of believers?

As a teacher, the community I interacted with the most consisted of fellow educators, students, and parents; thus, I was concerned about the legacy I and fellow educators were leaving behind. Having retired for now from teaching, I have come to realize an urgent need: all of us who name Christ as our Savior have the God-given responsibility to leave a legacy of Christlikeness.

Before addressing some further insights about Christendom today, I wish to share some valuable lessons from the past. I am forever a teacher, always striving to provide valuable lessons. The measurements of a lesson's success are recall and application. In other words, successful lessons stick.

The lessons I share in this book are not from brick-and-mortar class-rooms but from the lives of family members.

I dedicate this book to my maternal and paternal grandparents, my father, and my mother—who all impacted me for Christ.

In their shadows, I have a godly inheritance.

PART I

The Shadows in Which I Stand

CHAPTER 1

The Shadow Question: Are We Casting a Shadow of Christlikeness for Our Children?

EPIPHANIES ARE SUDDEN UNDERSTANDINGS. I HAD SUCH AN AWAK-ening some time ago amid my daily, morning routine. I like to start each day being in the know, so after spending some precious time in the Word and devotions each morning, I read various news articles to keep abreast of the issues of the day. On occasion, I like to read the thoughts of a liberal writer. My friends always ask, "Why?" The answer comes as no surprise to me: I like to argue, to express an opinion, and to show evidence to support that claim.

I say I do not like competition, and in some ways I don't, but deep inside I am a competitor. I like a good fight. One especially vocal writer, who shall remain nameless, stirs my juices. Her wide-open, full-throttle liberal comments, I confess, anger me at times. But mostly, they make me take stock of where I stand on contemporary issues and incite me to counterclaim her points of view. That, as much as I hate to admit it, is good journalism!

One day her article addressed the political future of the then upcoming 2020 presidential election. She examined the candidates and had come upon some enigmas in the political scene. Her questions raised troubling issues for me as well. Further thought caused me to ponder the relationship between her view of the waning political influence and my view of the waning effect of the church—the body of believers.

She asked why her political party did not foster young candidates—bright, energetic, cogent members of the party. Why were the loyalties of the party directed toward, shall we say, more *mature* leadership? She asked the question: What are we afraid of?

I have the same question regarding our children who have been entrusted to us: What are *we* afraid of?

Here is one example of what I mean. A dear friend of mine has a son who just graduated from college in computer technology. The university endorsed him as a viable candidate for the workplace. He is a bright, energetic, and persuasive new member of the professional arena. However, one problem exists: he cannot find a job.

Why? All the jobs require experience. The proverbial question becomes, how can he achieve experience if he cannot garner a job? What happened to the concept of entry-level positions that allow young candidates to follow experienced employees who then train the CEOs of the future? Why doesn't the workforce leadership trust the young people who have just come through training exceedingly above the education of our day? What are the companies afraid of?

The result of this travesty is that the young man is returning to school for his master's degree. The even sadder commentary is that when he finishes his master's program, the same hard truth will occur. He still will have no experience.

In the church community, we—the mature ones of the faith—often dig in our heels when any mention of a contemporary change comes about: projection screens, contemporary Christian music, worship leaders, or upstart deacons. While I am not saying that the young people's views should be the only views followed, I am saying that we should welcome and encourage their involvement in the church.

Many people, however, believe that young people—young couples, singles, and teens—should have no say in what goes on in certain ministries of the church. After all, *we* were not allowed to embrace the new songs of our day, to follow the new artists, or to have a voice in the workings of the church.

Many of us were not even allowed to express our thoughts. Children, in my day, were to remain quiet in church. Period. We were to absorb and sing only the hymns of the faith, even though they might not be biblical. Church leaders instructed us in some preferential doctrine, such as dress, degrees of sin, race, and so forth. I could name countless other preferential dictates, but exasperation prevents me from doing so.

Those of us who now represent the older generation in our churches often oppress our children in the same way we were oppressed. Why? Out of spite? Out of loyalty to our traditions? Out of the belief that our children should pay their dues?

Again, what are we afraid of? Don't we trust our youth?

The more disconcerting question may be harder for us to answer because it points to our weakness, so let me soften the blow by using the popular TV game show *Jeopardy* to pose the crux of the matter. The clue in the $1,000 dollar bracket would read: We have failed to do our job in providing a consistent example of Christ before our children. The troubling answer: What is yes?

Thus, we must further ask ourselves if we have been faithful to God. Are we committed to following Christ in our daily lives? What biblical instruction have we taught with our mouths and not lived out with our lives? What examples of Christlikeness have we portrayed to our children? What saintly virtues have we admittedly—like David, Jonah, Abraham, and others—mixed with carnal natures? Do we come clean with our children and admit when we are wrong? Or do we gloss over our sins—or, even worse, tolerate them—while adamantly condemning the sins of others in front of our children?

The liberal writer I spoke of earlier happily concluded that all was not lost for her party. Young governors, congresspeople, and party workers were on the rise. Maybe not in the coming election, but a young JFK was somewhere out there waiting to emerge. The party, she concluded, must show them the way, instruct them in the modern political methods, support them in their endeavors, and step aside so that they could advance to leadership. In her vernacular, the liberal party must train them in the way they should go. We are no less commanded by God in Proverbs 22:6 to do the same: "Train up a child in the way he should go; and when he is old, he will not depart from it." If the liberal writer can come to this viable conclusion, I can too. We Christians must show the young church—the young body of believers—the way. We must leave them a godly heritage and cast the right shadows.

The patriarchs of my family, though certainly not perfect, showed me "the way, the truth, and the life" (John 14:6) that I needed to live in this present age. Though all of them are now with their heavenly Father, their instruction still sustains me today.

In the following pages, we will draw some conclusions together. Let me step into their shadows for a while. Will you join me?

CHAPTER 2

Mis'ress Mabel, Do You Have Anything to Spare?

I NEVER KNEW MY MOTHER'S MOTHER. SHE DIED OF TUBERCULOSIS when my mother was ten and her brother was two. My mom's memories of her mother were minimal, so I know her through old pictures—a slender, brown-haired, brown-eyed woman with a humble presence. If I place early pictures of my mother beside pictures of my grandmother, I can't tell the difference.

Grandmother Mabel grew up in Narrows, Virginia, a quiet, small town nestled in the mountains where the New River narrows between East River Mountain and Peters Mountain. She bore her children during the Depression when few had anything luxurious, especially in Narrows. She knew the Lord and loved her husband and children; Mom testified to that.

Times were hard in the thirties, but Grandmother Mabel came from hearty stock, some of it Native American. From her parents, Laura and John Lamb, she learned resilience and solid faith in God and to make do with whatever she had. Regardless of the scarcity of food, the family never went to bed hungry. Grandmother always figured out some way to make "something out of nothing."

She sewed my mother's dresses from the fabric of her own or from Grandpa's pants and shirts that had grown threadbare. She worked in the town's laundry for fifteen cents an hour until her health would not permit her to work any longer. Her faith in God and loyalty to her husband were her sustaining graces.

My grandmother believed she should never turn away anyone from her door. She held firmly to Hebrews 13:1–3: "Let brotherly love continue. Be not forgetful to entertain strangers: for thereby some have entertained angels unawares. Remember them that are in bonds, as bound with them; and them which suffer adversity, as being yourselves also in the body."

During these troublesome times, *tramps*—so named in those days— would ride the railcars looking for work. They'd lodge under a bridge or a tree on some vacant property along the way and hire out for a day or two as they found temporary work. Things were no different in Narrows. The rail line was not far from my grandparents' home, so these homeless men were often in the neighborhood.

My grandparents had what was known as a shotgun house. Two rooms faced the street with four more rooms in the back, so the house looked something like this: front porch, living room and front bedroom, bedroom and bedroom, dining room and kitchen. All the rooms were incredibly small by today's standards.

At the back of the house was the summer kitchen, which was a small porch screened in for the smaller wood cookstove. Since no one had heard of air conditioning in those days, people could cook in the summer kitchen without heating up the house. Using that stove, Grandmother did the laundry and the summer canning and also cooked the evening meals. She made *cathead* biscuits; she squeezed off the dough from a roll instead of rolling out and cutting the dough with a biscuit cutter. These biscuits, shaped like cat heads, baked up fluffy. Together with other staples, like pinto beans and stewed tomatoes, she kept the family going. I am sure the aroma of canned beef or fatback and fried potatoes would waft across the yards from that summer kitchen.

Before long, as the smell of "something from nothing" drifted through the air, some of the men made their way to her back door.

With hats in hands, they'd ask, "Mis'ress Mabel. You have anything to spare?"

My grandmother would tell them to take a seat on the stone wall that bordered the backyard. Grandmother would never let the men enter the house because of her children, but she also never let any of them go away hungry. Maybe they would only receive a plate of pinto beans, a hunk of cornbread, and a glass of milk, but they would receive something.

My mom remembered that Grandmother Mabel always said grace with them before they ate. Her selflessness and humble spirit cast a giant shadow on my mother.

My mother walked in that shadow. When I was growing up, many times my mom, dad, and I would not sit down to a Thanksgiving meal or a Christmas dinner until Mom had made the rounds in the community.

She would fix and bake all day Wednesday to make ready the Thanksgiving boxes. Days before Christmas, she would begin packing bushel baskets with goodies. We would load the boxes—stuffed with turkey or ham, mashed potatoes, green beans, caramelized fried sweet potatoes, fresh bread, and a pumpkin or hickory nut pie—and distribute them around our little village of Mudsoc, Ohio.

First, we'd visit the Wiltodd brothers. As far as I know, they never talked to each other, but they talked with my mother. They literally had a line drawn down the middle of their log house; one sat at the window, and one sat at the door, even in winter. We always packed extra canned Mason jars of fruits and vegetables in their boxes.

Next, we would visit the Roses. They were an elderly couple whose family had moved away and ignored them for the most part. Mom's hickory nut pie was their favorite (pecans were a luxury, but hickory nut trees were in abundance on the farm).

Mr. Rose would always reward me with pink disk candies. They tasted like Pepto Bismol, and I could not abide them, but I always graciously took them and later gave them to my grandpa. Mother taught me to never refuse a gift or grimace at one and to always receive it with grace.

One giant shadow still lingering with me today is a Thanksgiving visit to the Green's house. (The names have been changed to protect the family's privacy.) Lee Green was my school friend from third grade. She had five brothers and sisters. Her mother, Ruth, was dying of cancer.

We arrived at the house, and Lee's dad met us at the door. The little ones hid behind his legs and peeped around at us. Lee stood apart and kept her head bowed—I wonder to this day what was going through her mind.

Mother took me in with her to speak with Ruth. What a death-like visage she had. When Mother told her that we had brought their Thanksgiving meal, tears rolled down her cheeks. She was incapable of cooking or providing a meal for her family. Her overflow of gratitude, and my mom's love for Ruth, permeated the room.

We went to the sparse kitchen to lay out the meal. Mother told me to get the plates, but I could not find enough.

When I told Mother, she said, "That's all right. Look around and see what you can find."

That day, we served Thanksgiving dinner to a family of eight on mismatched plates and pan lids. Mother's commitment to serving others reflected her mother's legacy of never turning a person in need from her door.

Because of my grandmother Mabel's legacy to my mother, and Mother's to me, I came to understand Jesus's words in Matthew 25:35–40 (ESV):

> "For I was hungry and you gave me food, I was thirsty and you gave me drink, I was a stranger and you welcomed me, I was naked and you clothed me, I was sick and you visited me, I was in prison and you came to me." Then the righteous will answer him, saying, "Lord, when did we see you hungry and feed you, or thirsty and give you drink? And when did we see you a stranger and welcome you, or naked and clothe you? And when did we see you sick or in prison and visit you?" And the King will answer them, "Truly, I say to you, as you did it to one of the least of these my brothers, you did it to me."

For you see, when we serve or receive others in their need, we are welcoming the Lord as well.

I believe that if I could have stood tall enough on that Thanksgiving Day, I could have seen my grandmother Mabel's shadow following Mother as we left the Green's home.

When it was finally time for our own meal, the dinner never tasted so good! I learned the beauty of being blessed more by giving than receiving.

I inherited my understanding of giving selflessly, walking in the shadow of my grandmother, Mabel Lamb.

CHAPTER 3

The Lord Giveth and the Lord Taketh Away

WHILE GRANDPA LEE COULD HAVE HARDLY CAST A TALL SHADOW, being only about five ten, his faith in God provided comfort for my mother.

It was July 10, the hottest day of the summer of 1934. The temperature was, as they say, "110 in the shade," only this time, it was literally 110. To make the day more dismal, my mother's mother, Mabel Lamb, was dying of tuberculosis.

The doctors could do nothing more for her, and the family had gathered on the front porch and steps of the shotgun house in Narrows, Virginia. Carrying her two-year-old brother around on her hip, my mother tried to answer his questions and to keep him occupied while the family talked in low voices. Mom headed toward the cherry trees in the backyard, hoping to gather some to satisfy her brother's whining demands.

As she rounded the corner of the house, her brother still on her hip, she noticed that the cow in the back pen was staggering. Somehow, she managed to run to the porch to tell her dad—my grandpa Lee—what she had seen. He came running just as the cow dropped to the ground. It died shortly thereafter. He put his arm around her shoulders and guided her back to the house, trying to answer the whys of two young children.

Later in the afternoon, Mom's uncle Russell Lamb called for Grandpa from the summer kitchen. The hog that the family was depending upon for food for the winter was struggling as well. Grandpa came running once again. This time he had to retrieve his rifle to put the suffering animal out of its misery. Two animals, necessary to sustain life in the Depression era of the thirties, were gone. A family member called for the vet, who arranged to remove the dead animals.

By early evening, it became clear that Grandma Mabel would soon go home to be with the Lord. The doctor arrived in time to officially pronounce her deceased.

And so, on July 10, 1934, three things that sustained the life of the Parcell family were gone: the family's milk cow, the family's hog, and the family's matriarch, Mabel Lamb Parcell. Left behind were a husband, a ten-year-old daughter, and a two-year-old son. My mother's memory of that day—painful and disjointed as it was—resounded with the exceedingly clear voice of her father.

Standing on the steps of the summer kitchen and watching as men hauled a dead cow and hog onto a truck, Grandpa Lee put his arm around my mother's shoulder and said, "The Lord giveth, and the Lord taketh away; blessed be the name of the Lord."

Grandpa's reference was from Job 1:21, which reads, "Naked came I out of my mother's womb, and naked shall I return thither: the LORD gave, and the LORD hath taken away; blessed be the name of the LORD." The previous verse reads, "Then Job arose, and rent his mantle, and shaved his head, and fell down upon the ground, and worshipped."

Job had lost all—his wealth and his children. Only his wife remained, and she discouraged rather than encouraged him. Grandpa Lee was left with two children to raise and a dismal outlook for the coming fall to winter, yet he never let his children see the hopelessness that many of us would have felt under the same tragic circumstances.

That day, my mother's father cast an enormous shadow that would shelter my mom through many heartbreaks, the most devastating of which were the loss of a child and her dear husband.

I was an only child in the fall of 1957. Dad called me into the living room from playing. He and Mom had some news to share. I remember jumping up and down and exclaiming joyfully my excitement when Mom and Dad told me that I was to have a new baby brother or sister. For seven years my parents had waited for this miracle! Dad, of course, wanted a boy. Mom wanted a healthy child, boy or girl, but shared that a girl and a boy would be a nice balance. And I wanted a baby sister. Boys, in my mind, were disgusting! Since the means of determining the gender of an unborn baby had not yet been developed, we would need to wait patiently for the baby to make an appearance before we knew who received their wish.

In the meantime, Mom and I made plans for his or her arrival. We moved the bassinet, which held my dolls and stuffed animals, from my room to Dad and Mom's room. Mom made a new liner to fit, and I found a little pillow that would complement the bedding. I told all my school friends, and Mom shared the news with family members and friends. They all responded with well-wishes and gifts. The church community had a shower for Mom, and I blissfully assisted in opening the presents. Much to my delight, most of the gifts were pink or my favorite color, yellow, both of which were the favored colors for a baby girl. Among the treasured items was an adorable little blue dress and a rosebud bedecked pink sweater. I could just imagine how beautiful my new sister would be in those clothes.

As the months passed and anticipation grew, Mom, Dad, and I talked of names for the baby. Dad avoided any consideration of passing down his name—Clarence Armet—to a son. His name was his name, and he didn't want to saddle anyone else with it. Mom was equally in agreement that LaVerne Lee would not be shared with this child, although Dad thought Lee would make a good middle name, boy or girl. They considered James after my grandfather Stewart and Lee after my grandfather Parcell. Susan, my grandmother Stewart's middle name, became the family pick for a girl; however, all of us liked other nonfamily names as well. I seem to remember that Matthew Todd was a chosen name for the boy. I wanted Judy or Trixie; Trixie was from a children's book series whose lead character was Trixie Belden. Dad quickly nixed that idea! Both Mom and Dad thought Judy to be a possibility, but it just didn't work with middle name choices. Dad and Mom liked the name Gail, mostly because they knew a sweet lady named Gail. Finally we all agreed on Judith Gail Stewart for a little girl. I don't remember the final boy's name because this baby was not to be a boy, according to my thinking.

With a name chosen, all that remained was to await the coming event. I don't remember much about the ensuing days except that I stayed confident the new addition would be a girl. I remember stopping often in the bedroom to gaze on the array of baby necessities stored in the bassinet or tucked in the dresser nearby. I could imagine all the things my sister and I would do together. I didn't consider in those times that play would be something I would need to wait for until she was old enough. I never, ever considered that I would be a teenager when she was five. I did imagine that only I would wheel my little sister around in the baby carriage. In my young mind, I was all ready to be the perfect older sister.

A couple of days before the due date, my mother went to Dr. Brown, our family doctor, for a final checkup. I stayed with a neighbor friend while Dad and Mom made the trip to town. Later that day, Dad stopped by to ask if Shirley, our neighbor, could keep me with her for the night. Dr. Brown had some concerns and had ordered Mom to be admitted to the hospital. I didn't know the full circumstances of those concerns until some years later. On June 7, 1958, Dr. Brown pronounced the "most beautiful baby girl" stillborn at Holzer Hospital in Gallipolis—the same doctor and the same hospital of my birth. I, on that day, became an only child once again.

I don't remember much about the hours and days after the birth of Judith. I remember that Mom stayed in the hospital for a day or two. I don't remember the details of how I was told of my sister's stillbirth or what that term even meant. I only remember that I was inconsolable! I know that when I cried in my dad's presence, he, too, cried. Oddly, my mom did not shed tears. She had only a look of compassion as I wailed out my sorrow.

I remember that I stayed at the home of my best friend, Linda, for a couple of weeks while Dad and Mom packed away the baby things and attempted to return to normal. I remember crying often and my friend telling me to stop crying so much. I, no doubt, screamed out that she had not lost a sister! Only after Mom sat down with me and explained that Judith was with Jesus in heaven did I reconcile the fact. Although I don't remember her exact words, I am sure that she relayed that Judith had been the Lord's and she had returned to Him. Nevertheless, I remember being comforted by her words of love.

It was on one of our movie night discussions years later that Mom shared the details of Judith's birth. Dr. Brown had been concerned because of the baby's faint heartbeat. Since machines echoing the heartbeat were not available in those days, Dr. Brown could only conjecture as to the condition of the baby. Mother shared her grief with the Lord and my father during those hours before Judith's birth. When Judith arrived, Dr. Brown had described her as a beautiful baby with no visible means of trauma. Without an autopsy, the cause of her death could not be determined. Mom and Dad decided that her beautiful little body would not be disfigured by such a procedure. By the time Mom returned home, her tears had run dry. I remember being in awe of my mom once again—her quiet resolve to accept this great loss.

That night she reminded me again of two important biblical facts: first and foremost, Judith was with the Lord in heaven. Second, the Lord gives and He takes away. His name is blessed in all circumstances and worthy of trust in all circumstances. This loss would be another of life's setbacks for my mother, but her resolve would always be the same.

Mom had lost her mother at a young age, and she lost her stepmother shortly after I was born. These losses, however, did not compare to the loss of her father, Lee Parcell.

To say my grandfather doted on his daughter would be an understatement. I don't mean that he gave her everything she wanted; he could not have even if he had wanted to. He never accumulated the wealth such indulgence would have required, but he gave her an abundance of love, his spoken pride in her life choices, and a biblical foundation that sustains.

When my grandfather left this earth, he left in the arms of his son. Uncle Herman was visiting with my grandfather and step-grandmother when Grandpa Lee walked into the living room, groaned slightly, and pitched over. Walking beside Grandpa, my uncle was able to catch him on the way to the floor—immediately absent from the body and present with the Lord. (Interestingly enough, my mother went home to be with her Lord in my arms. She, too, made a slight sound and pitched over; I caught her on the way to the floor as well. Coincidence? I think not.)

I was teaching in a university in South Carolina when I received the call from Mom that Grandpa Lee was with the Lord. Mom and Dad were on their way to Virginia from Ohio, and I would meet them there the next day. I wasn't with Mom during the hours after she received the urgent call, so I cannot relate what conversations or actions ensued. But knowing Mom, I am confident that she had not doubted for one moment the sovereignty of God in taking her father home. Since my mother's voice had been calm and reserved on the phone—no tears—I knew she had already committed her father into God's hands and was giving all glory to God for the privilege it had been to call Grandpa Lee "Father." Although Mom didn't say the words the day of the funeral, the joy amid the sorrow registering on her face assured me that the Lord gives and the Lord takes away; blessed be the name of the Lord (Job 1:21).

Her bequeathing of his message to me has sustained me through life's difficulties as well. When Satan tempts me to think life is too hard or, even worse, to whine over the trivial losses in this life, I return to Grandpa Lee's message, and it renews my hope.

I wonder if we could respond in the same way today if we suffered similar situations, such as the loss of a home, a financial advantage, and a loved one . . . all in the same day. Could we look at the circumstances of our lives and respond, "The Lord giveth, and the Lord taketh away"? Is there a shadow of confidence in God in which we can stand and, thereby, bequeath that same confidence to our children?

CHAPTER 4

The Ugliest Man in Giles County

GRANDPA LEE PARCELL HAD A DISTINCTIVE LOOK. A TUFTED RING of reddish-gray hair encircled his otherwise bald head. Brown freckles surrounded a distinctive nose. He was of average height, but his girth was as prominent as his nose. He often remarked that he kept an eye on his eating; he kept it right there where he could see it. He did love to eat, challenging many a family member to a lemon meringue pie eating contest (provided it was my mother's lemon pie).

The more winning aspect of him, however, was his smile, which readily occupied his face. One could easily say that he looked at life as half full instead of half empty. Although circumstances had not been kind to him from the world's standpoint (he had lost two wives to difficult illnesses), his face would never betray any heartache or sense of bitterness. He met everyone with a smile of assurance. That assurance came from knowing the Lord Jesus Christ as his Savior.

A man of modest means, he never demanded anything of the Lord. He was not showy in his faith or eloquent in his speech regarding the Lord.

At meals he gave the same blessing. "Lord, Jesus, we truly thank thee. Thou abidest us all and have saved us from sin for Christ's sake. Bless this food in Jesus's name. Amen."

The words became so familiar to him and run together that often-times family members had to interpret the encrypted message for others.

Grandpa Lee did not have wealth or property. In fact, he trusted everyone he met and everything they said, which tormented my step-grandmother, Veta. Because of his gullibility, he would trade his best car, knife, gun, or some other item of value for one of lesser quality. He accepted everyone just the way he met them. I often think of the Lord when I think of Grandpa Lee, for the Lord meets all men and women just the way they are. He, of course, does not leave them there, but He welcomes them as they are, nonetheless.

Grandpa Lee did not have a high societal position. He was a hard-working man, employed at the local laundry during the Depression. He also drove a milk truck at one time, worked at the local tannery for years, and finally worked at and retired from the Celanese Corporation in Pearisburg, Virginia, just outside the town in which he grew up and raised his own family.

Grandpa Lee's claim to fame happened quite by accident. The Giles County Fair was a regular summer event. It had agricultural exhibits, amusement rides, livestock showings, and various other attractions. Among the many contests—queen crowning, food eating, and other contestable activities—was the "Ugliest Man in Giles County" contest. On a dare, no doubt from one of his brothers, my grandfather entered the contest and won. His name and picture with his trophy appeared in the local newspaper. Surprisingly, what would have mortified most people was a door of opportunity for my grandfather. He often opened a conversation with a total stranger by saying, "Hello, I'm Lee Parcell, voted the ugliest man in Giles County!"

After a hearty, eye-to-eye handshake, a conversation would ensue, and before long some mention of the Lord would be made. I don't know if anyone ever came to know the Lord because of his moniker, but I do know that he used it as an opportunity to witness. I also know that he talked to and prayed for all his family members until one by one he saw them accept the Lord as their Savior.

My grandfather went to be with the Lord in June of 1978. When the pastor met with my mother, her brother, and my step-grandmother to discuss the funeral arrangements, he asked if he could use the famous nickname for Grandpa Lee as the opening to his sermon. He felt it seemed fitting somehow. Both women and my uncle agreed.

I was not prepared at the funeral for the width or breadth of the shadow my humble grandfather had engendered across the modest town and county. I was awestruck by the number of people who came to pay tribute to the eighty-something-year-old man and the kind words they shared with the family.

More astounding was the message the pastor gave, with the foundation based on Proverbs 22:1: "A good name is rather to be chosen than great riches, and loving favour rather than silver and gold." He followed that verse with another, Ecclesiastes 7:1: "A good name is better than precious ointment; and the day of death than the day of one's birth."

My grandfather was the oldest of his siblings, and there had always been murmur as to his heritage. He had overcome the stigma of a questionable birth, however, by his strong character and his care for his siblings in their times of need.

The pastor opened the sermon by making mention of Grandpa's pride in being the ugliest man in Giles County before expanding his thoughts that Grandpa's true winning name was his integrity, his accepting kindness, and his love for the Lord. His name was better than great riches and more precious than costly ointment. Grandpa Lee glorified God with an unblemished name.

The physical inheritance that came from my grandpa Lee was a pocket watch, a wristwatch given to him by the Celanese plant, a shotgun and rifle, a table radio that he prized, and a modest sum of money to his son and daughter. More importantly, he bequeathed to them a name, which was highly favored.

I stand in the shadow of an inheritance from Grandpa Lee that instructed me in the importance of one's reputation—not societal position, wealth, or fame—but in having a good name that speaks to others of the greater name of Christ Jesus.

CHAPTER 5

The Master Is Come and Calleth for Thee

VETA WAS THE ONLY MATERNAL GRANDMOTHER I EVER KNEW. SHE married my grandpa Lee when I was three years old. She was Grandpa's third wife, and he was her second husband. Both had lost their dearly loved spouses, and both brought their own children to the marriage.

Veta was a trip. At scarcely five feet tall, she wore Mary Janes because she could not find grown-up shoes to fit her size four-and-a-half feet. She grew up in Narrows, and her entire world consisted of that community and the nearby towns. She never traveled anywhere significantly until she married my grandpa.

To her, our home in Ohio was Mecca. The first time she came with Grandpa Lee to visit us was the first time, to my knowledge, that she crossed the borders of three states: Virginia, West Virginia, and Ohio. She believed everything was bigger and better in Ohio.

For one thing, in Gallipolis, Ohio, Carl's Shoe Store had ladies' shoes that would fit her. For another, Gallipolis had a Bob Evans Steak House. It was the original Bob Evans restaurant, owned and operated by the original Bob Evans, a born-and-bred Gallia countian. She had never tasted restaurant food like that!

When we would send Mother's Day corsages to her in Virginia, the florist required a minimum ten-dollar order to wire flowers, so the corsage would be particularly large. She would tell everyone that Ohio flowers were bigger and better than what the shops had in Narrows, not understanding that the flowers had come from the local florist in Narrows.

When I was a toddler and old enough to recognize that Veta was my grandmother, I had an instant bond with her. This bond largely came because she made a place for me in her home and in her heart.

My parents and I had journeyed to Virginia for a visit. I was too big for a bassinet, and no such thing as a portable crib existed. I could have slept with Dad and Mom, but Dad feared his six-foot-plus frame would crush me if he turned over.

Veta came to the rescue. She took the two stuffed living room chairs and pushed them together front to front. She covered them with a sheet and packed a blanket tightly within the gaps between cushions and chairs. Mother provided my little bed pillow that had traveled with me. I remember feeling like a queen in my special bed, lovingly prepared by my step-grandmother.

Grandmother Veta simply became Veta to me that weekend and remained my Veta until the day God took her home. As for Mother, she never felt that Veta was anything but a mother to her and a wife to her dad. She never saw Veta as an intruder into her relationship with her father. Their bond was love.

When people saw Grandpa Lee and Veta in their car, they would see two heads instead of one on the driver's side. In the early days, cars had bench seats, and Veta would scoot over next to Grandpa. That was the way she insisted they travel. This practice became the source of much teasing—two love birds old enough to be grandparents to most of the world's population, sitting like teenagers all snuggled up together.

Curious, I once asked Veta, "Why do you sit so closely to Grandpa? Is it safe?"

She explained, "If we are ever in a car wreck, Lee isn't going anywhere without me!"

Like so many members of my mother's family, Veta was not self-affronting. She was hard working and humble, the same as my grandfather. Most of us marveled at the pace at which she did everything . . . generally a run. If we wanted to help her, we had better be prepared to run too. Her signature attire was a full-bibbed apron, which she wore constantly around the house to keep her other clothes from receiving the brunt of a hard day's canning or working in the garden. If she needed to carry something, the apron became a soft-sided basket.

By Veta's side, I learned to make biscuits in a wash pan, complete with a good helping of lard and a "well" in the middle full of buttermilk. While they were not the cathead biscuits my mother made, they were just as filling and just as good. I learned that a glass rim dipped in buttermilk and flour made a great biscuit cutter. While we made biscuits or home-made custard pie or stirred stovetop rhubarb preserves, we talked of love and family and life.

There's a well-known expression: Bibles that are coming apart are carried by people who are not. Veta's Bible was tattered and well-worn. No one questioned that she knew the Lord personally and knew Him well. She lived out her understanding before others.

After my grandfather died, Veta lived with her brother Jesse until God took him home as well. Then she moved into a small house close to one of her sons.

We bought special things for her for Christmas, and when we visited, we'd notice that she was not using those things. One day she took Mom and me into her bedroom and opened a wooden chest. There lay a beautiful pink nightgown with satin, lace, and rose trimmings that we had bought her. Beside it was a beautifully crocheted shawl with deep front pockets in an intricate open-work design. I had bought both of my grandmothers one for Christmas. That day she gave us strict instructions that she was to wear that gown and shawl for her funeral service. She relayed that her own mother had been dressed in similar fashion when she died, and Veta had the same desires.

"Going home to heaven will be like lying down to sleep in the arms of Jesus," Veta said.

In early September 1988, half a year after her eighty-fourth April Fool's Day birthday, we received a call from her son Bill. Veta had gone home to be with her Lord. Bill said that he had checked on her that morning and had found her sitting in her favorite chair. She had removed the apron she always wore, as if her work on earth was through, and had draped it over the chair. She had her Bible in her lap, her finger poised over John 11:28: "The Master is come and calleth for thee." This is found in the story of the death and resurrection of Lazarus and the meeting of Jesus with his two sisters.

These verses precede that noted verse: "Jesus said unto her, I am the resurrection, and the life: he that believeth in me, though he were dead, yet shall he live: and whosoever liveth and believeth in me shall never die" (John 11:25–26).

Because Veta believed these verses, her life had only just begun.

Veta bequeathed to me the understanding that we celebrate the home-going of a person in Christ; we do not mourn their death, for death is but the passage to eternal life. True, we sorrow over the loss and absence that we will feel, but we celebrate the undeniable fact that our loved ones in Christ are not in the grave but are with Him in glory.

The viewing and funeral of Veta Smith Parcell was a continual testimony of God's presence with us. We complied with Veta's wishes and made sure she was dressed in the pink gown and embraced by the white crocheted shawl. But that was not all. We carefully arranged a Bible with her fingers lying upon it and pointing to the very verse to which her Bible had lain open. All who were there that day—saved and unsaved—read those verses Veta had left behind as her testimony of God's ministering grace.

What a giant shadow for such a petite lady. What a legacy!

CHAPTER 6

Come All Ye Who Are Weary

SINCE I WAS THE YOUNGEST GRANDCHILD ON MY FATHER'S SIDE of the family, my grandmother was already sixty-nine years old when I was born. Unlike my mother's mother and stepmother, my grandmother Tacy was a proud woman—not in an offensive way but in a confident way.

First, she was proud of her name: Tacy Susan. I have not known another Tacy in all my days. Second, she was proud of her stature, both in physical form and in the family lineup. She was the third of seven girls and by far the prettiest of the lot. She didn't say so, but Aunt Sarah Jane—her older sister—did! (Aunt Sarah Jane was so jealous that she once cut off Grandma's hair. It was the only time Grandma could remember having her hair significantly cut.)

Grandmother Tacy was tall and big boned but in a statuesque way. Her hair was platinum blond at birth, and it remained so until she contracted the measles in her twenties, which turned her golden hair pure white. Nevertheless, her waist-length white hair was her crowning glory. She wore it woven into figure eights and rolled until it made a wonderful crown around the sides and back of her head. She looked every bit the Gibson girl of the turn of the 1900s. Her penetrating blue eyes held a touch of mischief, and her smile was warm and welcoming. She never went to town or to church without a hat and gloves. She was a beautiful woman both inside and out.

Grandma Stewart had a green thumb and a command of animals, able to tame both weed and ornery critter with ease. She once felt betrayed by her pet duck because she thought he had pecked the back of her leg. Later she was surprisingly glad to discover it was actually a blood clot. The sudden pain had not been an attack by her favorite drake. She trained her cat to do tricks like a dog and took pride in having the cat perform for visitors, mildly scolding when the cat was contrary.

My favorite summer pastime with her was potting leaves or seeds collected from her favorite flowers. She would show me how to plunge my thumb into the dark soil, stick the seed or leaf's stem just below the surface, cover it over or surround it with dirt, and give it a loving pat. I have many pictures of three- or four-year-old me with Grandma and our clay pots of budding plants.

Since so much of Grandma's early life is from my dad's memories, I can only relate the legacies that Grandma Stewart gave to him through his stories.

Grandma and Grandpa had a hill farm in southeastern Gallia County, Ohio, just below Mercerville. Because Depression times were hard, Grandpa became a traveling salesman, selling everything from pump organs to Rawleigh products, a conglomeration of medicinal remedies, cleaners, and baking goods. He would be gone weekdays, and Grandma and the boys—my dad's older brothers Oty and Arthur—would tend to the farm. By the time Dad was man enough to work the fields, Oty and Arthur were married and gone. Their absence left the field work to Grandma and Dad.

How the farm and the family could survive under such circumstances is hard to know, but survive it they did. When visitors came to call, Grandma could prepare a meal fit for royalty when groceries were scarce and money was even scarcer. How she could sing "What a Friend We Have in Jesus" when all around her seemed hopeless is almost miraculous. But sing she did!

My dad learned to walk in the shadow of his mother's work ethic. One tale impacted me the most: *the wet-shirt story.*

Just above the barn and across the gravel road lay an acre of field corn. The corn had to be hoed on a regular basis to keep weeds from taking over and to keep the soil loosened to produce a better crop. This hoeing did not come in the cool spring but, rather, in the sweltering summer. Grandma would equip Dad with the short-handled hoe, and she would take the long-handled one. She'd start at the far edge of the field and hoe toward him, while he took the road end.

Before the hoeing began, Grandma would say, "Clarency, if you hoe until your shirt is soaked through, you can have some tea and a lemon cracker." (Lemon crackers were square cookies Grandma managed to create out of a little lemon juice, sugar, lard, and cornmeal.) Since "real" cookies were a delicacy in those days, Dad was especially fond of those lemon crackers.

Dad was about ten or eleven at the time. He would work down his row until he thought his arms would break off. Then he'd run to his mother and ask if his shirt was wet enough yet. His shirt would be wringing wet, but Grandma would feel of his back, and say, "Not quite yet. Can you hoe one more row?"

Dad would run back and begin another row. By midmorning the two miraculously hoed out the field. Grandma would finally feel Dad's shirt and pronounce it wet enough. Then they would go to the house for the promised tea and lemon cracker.

As far as I know, Grandma never complained about running the farm while Poppy (her name for Grandpa Stewart) was away. If she did, Dad never mentioned it. She and my dad were made of solid stuff. My dad always worked hard to have that wet-shirt pronouncement at the end of the day.

As an adult, he owned a floor sanding business for thirty-three years, and his work ethic and integrity learned in the shadow of his mother established a reputation in our southeastern Ohio area. Grandma Tacy lived out, "Come to me, all who labor and are heavy laden, and I will give you rest. Take my yoke upon you, and learn from me, for I am gentle and lowly in heart, and you will find rest for your souls" (Matthew 11:28–29 ESV).

One of her legacies to me was to be able to lay my own head on my pillow at night and tell the Lord I had done my best for Him that day. That was one of Grandma's mantras, passed down to my dad, then passed down to me.

In a current society that minimizes effort, seeks shortcuts to success, and esteems leisure and comfort above all things, the wet-shirt-work-ethic appears to be waning. Those of us who earned the luxuries we enjoy seem to have a greater appreciation for them than those to whom the luxuries came without effort.

I prefer to stand in the shadow of a man who stood in the shadow of a woman who knew the value and, dare I say, pleasure of a hard day's work.

CHAPTER 7

In My Father's House
Are Many Mansions

MY GRANDMOTHER STEWART WAS A CHURCHGOER WHO CAME from a family of churchgoers. She and Grandpa met at church, dated at church, were—of course—married in church, and raised their family to go to church. Church was at the center of their world.

When a community of believers approached Grandpa about joining their endeavor to build a nondenominational country church, he and Grandma gladly agreed. It was to be a Bible-believing church without a denominational organization dictating the leadership. In those days, these country congregations had seen too much control levied over the community churches by the ruling organization, yet a percentage of the church's money was to go to the denomination's corporate fund. As I understand it, the situation was like taxation without representation.

When construction of the building ended, a quandary arose as to what to call it. The congregation struggled because even though it was Baptistic in doctrine, they did not want it to be Baptist in name. Though many of its members had been Methodist, it could not be Methodist in name either. Finally, the male leadership put the question to the congregation at large: Did anyone have a suggestion for a name?

My grandmother spoke up. "I think we should call it King Chapel."

Taking on the possessive form in the community's vernacular, the church became King's Chapel but still bearing the banner name King Chapel. That pure white country church sitting amid a grove of trees atop a hill in southeast Ohio became a beacon for that whole community. And yes, my grandmother was proud that the name she suggested hung above its doors.

The Bible was also at the center of the family's world. Grandma memorized whole passages of Scripture and recited them regularly to anyone who would sit still long enough to listen. Her favorite passage was John 14:1–3:

> Let not your heart be troubled: ye believe in God, believe also in me. In my Father's house are many mansions: if it were not so, I would have told you. I go to prepare a place for you. And if I go and prepare a place for you, I will come again, and receive you unto myself; that where I am, there ye may be also.

My grandfather died when I was thirteen, and my grandmother soon came to live with us. She was well into her eighties by then, and though she was physically strong, her mind was failing fast. She still, however, remembered whole passages of Scripture.

Her recitations would begin with, "I said . . . I said . . . In my father's house are many mansions . . ."

In the succeeding years, Grandma as we knew her was no longer there. The disease, known then as hardening of the arteries or today as dementia or Alzheimer's, spoke and acted for her. We were unrecognizable to her, and in her mind, we posed a threat because she had no memory of a grown Clarency with a wife and daughter. To her, Clarency was still a little boy.

God's grace is abundant to us even when we are no longer aware of Him. He amazes me the way He preserves His Word and allows His Word to spread in spite of dire circumstances. Grandma's only communication at the end of her days consisted of, "I said . . . I said . . . In my Father's house are many mansions. If it were not so, I would have told you. I go to prepare a place for you. And if I go and prepare a place for you, I will come again, and receive you unto myself; that where I am, there ye may be also."

Every nurse, doctor, and visitor heard that passage multiple times every single day. Though her body and mind were beyond human help, God kept His Word alive in her.

Arduous work, King's Chapel, and John 14—a shadow in which I am proud to stand!

CHAPTER 8

What About Your Soul?

JIMMY STEWART—NOT THE ACTOR BUT MY FATHER'S FATHER—WAS a gentle man. He, like my grandmother, was in his seventies when I first had recollection of him. He was slight of build and walked with a certain distinguishable gait. His hair, once red, was then snow white. His smile and chortle were a source of joy for those in his midst.

In the living room of my grandparents' modest clapboard home sat two rocking chairs, side by side and facing the fireplace. Many a day I sat on the floor in the space between them looking up at two spiritual giants. I say that for two reasons: in the light of the floor lamp, their images cast enormous flickering shadows on the fireplace-facing wall and the ceiling above, and between those two rockers I sat listening to them expound on the Bible, filling my little mind with a wondrous legacy of the Word of God.

My grandfather was gentle, except when it came to knowing about a person's soul; then he was a tenacious tiger. Grandpa never let a person leave his home without inquiring about his or her soul. For the family, his fondness for pinning a person to the wall, as they called it, became both a source of embarrassment and a source of pride.

Since my other cousins either lived far away or were married with their own families, I was the one most often privy to his sermonettes. Family and friends would come down to visit my family first and would then say that they wanted to go visit my grandparents. Since those days were prior to GPS, and these family members and friends clearly did not have a clue how to wind their way from our house to Grandma and Grandpa's house,

Dad would send me with them. I guided them along the country roads to their destination. Then, since seating was at a premium in the quaint living room, I'd take my usual position on the floor between the two chairs. There I would hear both Grandma and Grandpa speak the Scriptures vibrantly as they made the Old Testament saints come alive or explained the New Testament's parables and letters.

Oftentimes, the Scriptures were a continual narrative without any reference to which verses they were reciting. Grandpa just spoke the Word. The verses' locations were not as important as the Word and its impact. I memorized verses in that manner, and I believe that is why today I often know and quote Scripture without addresses.

The passage that was especially important to me early in my life was, "Behold, I stand at the door, and knock: if any man hear my voice, and open the door, I will come in to him, and will sup with him, and he with me." Even though it was a favorite known verse and a favorite picture on my Sunday school card, I didn't know its address (Revelation 3:20) until much later.

Grandpa always ended his explanation of Scripture with the proverbial question, "How is it with your soul?"

No escape was possible. Whoever was visiting either gave unmistakable evidence that he or she knew the Lord and followed His Word, or they were privileged to hear another challenge like the noteworthy John 3:16: "For God so loved the world, that he gave his only begotten Son that whosoever believeth in him should not perish, but have everlasting life." Or Grandpa would point out to some of our wealthier family members, "For what is a man profited, if he shall gain the whole world, and lose his own soul? or what shall a man give in exchange for his soul?" (Matthew 16:26). No one could ever say that he had never heard the Word if he had ever visited the Jim Stewart residence.

Grandpa did not stop talking about God and His Word when he walked out his front door. He accosted people on the streets of Gallipolis—not in a mean way, but he was so passionate about people coming to know Jesus as Savior that the place did not matter. What mattered was their knowing that they were sinners in need of a Savior. What also mattered was that someone cared enough about their eternal destiny that he did not care where or when the message was given; he only cared that it was boldly delivered.

I wish I had the same tenacity that I once had. Sitting in the shadow of my grandpa Jimmy, I learned boldness. It is no wonder that when I asked Jesus into my heart at not quite four years old, I walked down Second Avenue of Gallipolis, Ohio, telling everyone I met that I had been saved.

My next statement stemmed from an inheritance bold and sure: "Have you been saved?"

One man I met looked down at me with a tear in his eye and remarked, "Yes, young lady, I have been saved, but no one has ever asked me that question before." He then reached into his pocket and pulled out a quarter to give to me. I still have that quarter today.

Again, my paternal grandfather was not a tall man, scarcely five ten, as was my maternal grandfather, but the enormity of his witness was a shadow I could never exceed.

CHAPTER 9

And the Walls Came Tumbling Down

WHAT WOULD YOU DO IF YOU SAW A ONCE VIBRANT CHURCH empty and padlocked? Would you say, "What a shame," and move on, or would you be so grieved of heart that you simply had to see that something was done? For Brother Jim, as the community called him, the latter was without a doubt the response.

When times were hard, my grandfather Jim left the farm and became a door-to-door salesman. As a traveling salesman, he knew every road and route through Gallia County and parts of Lawrence County, Ohio. He traveled most of them on his sales runs.

One day he was traveling by horseback down a familiar road past Bethlehem Baptist Church. As he looked up at the steepled building sitting high on a hill, he caught a flash of light reflecting off something on the door. Curious, he rode up the sharp incline to the front of the church to find a padlock affixed to the door. A notice nailed to that door announced that it had been closed by the Baptist organization in charge of the church. Such a situation grieved my grandfather. He walked all around the church peeping in through the windows. The inside was intact, with every hymnal in place and the Bible still sitting on the Communion table.

He tried each of the windows until he found one that would open. The windows were several feet off the ground, but somehow Grandpa found a way to climb in. He was not there to take anything—he was there to pray. He never said how long he prayed, but knowing Grandpa, the prayer was long and impassioned.

This became a daily practice. He would stop on his route, crawl through the window, and kneel at the altar to pray the padlock off that church door.

His praying did not go unnoticed, but thankfully, not by the county sheriff, who could have arrested him for breaking and entering. People who walked by the church noticed and heard his voice echoing through the empty room. Men Grandpa knew well began to crawl through the windows to join him. Soon a large group began congregating for prayer. Those men, led by my grandfather, prayed for the lock to be taken off Bethlehem Baptist Church's door. And it was!

The men and their families soon started coming in the evenings. Someone would start a hymn, another would share a verse, someone else—oftentimes my grandfather—would expound upon the Word. Then a time of prayer and soul-searching would follow. A revival broke out in that once padlocked church that lasted six weeks, without one preacher, pastor, or evangelist . . . just a group of prayer warriors and the Holy Spirit. It must have been a little like the walls of Jericho. When the men shouted, the walls came tumbling down. When Grandpa Jim and the community prayed together, the walls of resistance and spiritual lostness came down!

Many years later, my dad, my mom, Grandpa Jim and Grandma Tacy, and Mary Wolford—a family friend who stayed with and cared for my grandparents—made a trip to four churches so important to Grandpa and Grandma in their lives: Victory Baptist Church (where they met), Siloam Baptist Church (I don't remember its importance), Bethlehem Baptist Church (the padlocked church), and finally King Chapel. Mom took pictures of the group in front of each church. All were still active except for Bethlehem, which, sadly, had lost its vibrancy and its congregation. The storms of life had knocked out its windows, stripped its paint, and caved in its roof with its bell tower. (The bell, I am told, became the device used to signal a touchdown at my high school alma mater.) Yet my grandfather once again reiterated the account of the widespread news of a revival in a church that had been padlocked.

After my father died, my mom and I traveled the not-so-familiar roads to those churches again. We were able, amazingly, to still find the sites of all the churches; both Victory and King Chapel still held services. We found only the foundation stones of Bethlehem, a few pieces of wreckage, and the old cemetery behind the church remaining. While the church lay in ruin, the souls saved in that church are not in ruin; they are with the God of heaven in whom they placed their trust.

To my knowledge no record was made of the number of people saved in that revival; only eternity will tell who came to know the Lord in those weeks. I learned from this relayed history passed down to me from my dad that the "effectual fervent prayer of a righteous man [men and women] availeth much" (James 5:16). My grandfather cared enough to stop by an old country church and pray for its "soul." The result was a miraculous spread of the gospel. My, what a shadow of an inheritance!

CHAPTER 10

The Cleft of the Rock

THE OLD STEWART PLACE SAT IN A NARROW GLEN BETWEEN TWO rugged hills. The only road into the homestead was a winding trail, wide enough for one vehicle in clear weather and narrow and muddy enough to require other modes of transportation if the weather warranted.

Three farms and Mooney schoolhouse were the only properties on that road. The last curve and crest of the hill before reaching my grandparents' home—the first of the farms—ran over a rock house, a cave-like structure hollowed out of solid rock. It was at this rock house that my grandfather prayed when his heart was heavily burdened over someone's lost soul or when life had presented yet another seemingly overwhelming trial.

Grandma thought nothing of Poppy leaving his hoe in the field and disappearing for an hour or longer, even though the chores had to be taken up by the rest of the family. She never complained because she knew where he was . . . at the rock house.

I had heard about the rock house most all my early life, as had my cousin Jim. But try as we might, we were never able to find the one trail out of so many that led to the gem hidden in a rock. Of course, as preteens, we were not permitted to leave the road to strike up the rugged hills on our own—even though we sometimes did. We were warned about copperheads and wild game, so we wouldn't venture far before we, or at least I, chickened out. The rock house remained, for us, uncharted territory. I only saw the rock house once in my life, and that visit is forged in my memory.

After my grandparents had long passed, Dad stopped going to the homeplace. I suppose nothing was left that he yearned to see. It came as a surprise one day when Dad "suggested" in his commanding way that we—Mom, Dad, and I—were going for a drive in the country. Dad had determined to go home again but by a more unusual way than we were accustomed. We would not be driving down the once familiar road or walking up the hill from the old smokehouse long gone. No, this time we were hiking in, down a trail unfamiliar to Mom and me. I now consider it a privilege to have taken that hike with Dad.

It was a fall Saturday afternoon. The air had been crisp and cold enough that threats of attacks by wild creatures were minimal. Just in case, Dad carried his pistol and a hatchet, should we need to clear some brush. We started at the top of the ridge across from Victory Baptist Church and headed down through Sheets' apple orchard. The trail was rough and, in some places, difficult to find, let alone navigate. But Mom and I kept Dad in sight, following in his footsteps and his *shadow* cast by the afternoon sun.

At this point, the trek was not my favorite idea that Dad had ever had. The scratches and bruises sustained in the brush did not help make it a pleasant experience. On more than one occasion, I wanted to turn back. I suspect my mother did as well, but I knew that I could have never found my way back and that this adventure was of supreme importance to Dad. Relinquishing my attitude, I determined to treat the journey like a treasure hunt. Only we had better find the treasure soon, or my negative attitude might return with a vengeance.

We arrived at a small clearing surrounded by a stand of trees. Through the brush to our left, we could make out the road's turn before its descent to the homeplace. I knew then of Dad's purpose in coming. Suddenly, the rock house came into view. I watched my dad slowly approach. Then he did a strange thing . . . he took off his cap.

Mother and I made our way to where he stood. The rock had a cleft to the left and a hollowed out opening immediately in front of us. I followed Dad's sight line to the floor of the rock house. There in the stone were two smooth indentations; something had worn away the stone. I knew someone's knees—my grandfather's—had met the floor of that cave in the exact same position over several years. I then understood why Dad had removed his cap. We were standing on holy ground. Dad relayed the familiar story of Grandpa and the rock house to us and then led us in a prayer of thankfulness for safety in finding the place and for the man God had raised up to pray for the souls of his family members, his friends, and those in that small community.

That story I knew so well was that a man had come to Victory Baptist Church one night during a revival. I only remember his first name: Jake. Jake was not a well-respected man. He was a moonshiner, and he had a reputation of being a mean drunk. His family suffered abuse, physically and financially, when he was drinking.

Most every Saturday night, he made his way on foot up the road to catch a ride to town and returned well into Sunday morning by that same route. Often when he arrived at the crest of the hill sometime around daybreak, he would hear a voice calling out his name. His name would echo across the valley, and each time, Jake stopped and listened, half out of fright and half out of bewilderment. That voice came from my grandfather, kneeling in prayer at the rock house. Jake's name, among many, rose to heaven from that sacred place.

On one particular occasion, Jake was so overcome by the passion of the pleading voice that he could stand it no longer. That night, as the story goes, Jake accompanied his wife to the revival service, walked down the aisle, and pled for the men, including my grandfather, to pray for his soul.

That night Jake came to know the Lord as his Savior.

As far as I know, Dad never returned to the rock house or drove by the farm after that day. I doubt that I could find the rock house from either the smokehouse or church trail, but I do imagine if I could follow that trail today, I would still find those two indentations embedded in the rock. In this case it is not the shadow that is my inheritance so much as it is the symbolism there; it is the cleft of a rock—the rock of Christ Jesus, in whose shadow my grandfather knelt and thankfully in whose shadow I rest today.

CHAPTER 11

A New Bride Adorned

DESPITE THE HARDSHIP AND LOSS SUFFERED IN MY MOTHER'S childhood years, in her teen years, life for LaVerne Lee Parcell, a slender, brown-haired, brown-eyed young woman from Narrows, Virginia, would dramatically change.

During the late thirties to early forties, LaVerne had practically raised her brother, with help from her widowed father and neighboring relatives; had graduated from high school; and had begun making her own money as an employee of the Celanese Corporation in nearby Pearisburg, Virginia.

By Mom's late teens, her dad had married Margie Lester, a strong-willed woman older than Mom's father. My mom found that she, at twenty-one, was no match for this new stepmother. As all young women do, Mom began longing for a place to call her own. Fortunately for her, Margie had many much younger siblings so close in age to Mom that they became more like brothers and sisters than aunts and uncles. One of those "brothers," Lacy, was in the Army Air Corps. Through him, Mom began writing to a soldier from Ohio who was in Lacy's company.

In those days, young women used all kinds of questionable methods to tell their future, especially in predicting whom they would marry. One idea was for a girl to take a hair from her head, drop it in a glass of water, and place the glass under her bed. In the morning, the hair would form the initial of the girl's future last name. On a dare from her best friend Dorothy, Mom went through the ritual. The next morning the hair formed an S, which just happened to be the first letter of the last name of the sergeant to whom she had been writing: Clarence A. Stewart.

Mom said right then and there, "I am going to marry that man!"

After WWII ended in 1945, Dad came to Virginia to meet Mom, and the rest is history. They were married on December 7, 1946. Much like Ruth in responding to Naomi, Mom believed, "For where you go, I will go, and where you lodge, I will lodge; your people shall be my people, and your God my God" (Ruth 1:16 ESV). Mom packed up all she had and moved with my dad to Huntington, West Virginia, where Dad had secured a job driving a bread truck for Mootz's Bakery (later to become Sunbeam Bakery). They lived in a two-bedroom upstairs apartment over a German couple's drug store. That dramatic change in Mom's life had just begun! Mom did not know very much about cooking or housekeeping, but the German lady adopted her and taught her much about how to make a home.

Mom had an effortless way about her that endeared her to people, even though she was somewhat shy. Dad introduced her to one of his cousins and his wife, who lived in Huntington and sang in a local quartet. Mack and his wife, Myrtle, became quick friends for the new bride. Mack encouraged Mom and Dad to sing together. Dad had that rich bass voice, and Mom sang "also." Mack named her voice as "also" because she sang alto part of the time and tenor the rest. Nevertheless, her voice moved people whenever she sang, largely because the joy from her heart radiated on her face.

After two years in West Virginia, Dad found a hill farm in Gallia County, Ohio. They moved to the farm at the head of Houck Hollow, off Peter Cave Road, just above Mudsoc, Ohio. Since Dad worked both on the farm and as a carpenter in Gallipolis, Mom took on many farm duties alone, but according to my dad, she never complained.

The farm wives in the community became fast friends for Mom. The Ladies Aide Society of Lincoln Ridge Methodist Church taught her to sew her own clothes, quilt, churn butter, stir off apple butter, and crochet.

Since Mom did not work outside the home, Dad gave Mom the left-over change from the grocery shopping, which she kept in the cookie jar. She was so proud when she had saved enough to buy a $2.98 house dress and a 98¢ rug for the kitchen. Mom became the model of a homemaker and farm wife.

Our local community church and the Stewart family suffered some culture shock with the newest Stewart member, however. Mother had grown up in the Pentecostal Holiness Church in Narrows, so at a revival meeting at Lincoln Ridge Church, Mother became slain in the spirit and spoke in tongues. The congregation was astir.

Dad looked down at Mom and simply said, "We don't do that here."

Mom never spoke in tongues again.

Not all her impact was of that nature, however. The first Christmas with my dad's parents was an eye-opener for Mom. There was no Christmas tree, decorations, or presents. The family's tradition since Dad had been a child was to give only stocking stuffers. When Mother saw the dearth of Christmas cheer, she sent Dad with an ax to cut the top from a pine tree. They went to town to buy a red cellophane candle wreath for the door, some tree lights, and a box of ornaments. A manger scene would be added another year.

That year was the first Christmas in my grandparents' home that the family exchanged boxed gifts. Grandma cried and declared that they should have been doing this all along.

Mom also introduced Dad to birthday cake on the first birthday he shared with his new wife. They took the leftover cake to Grandma and Grandpa's the following Sunday. Again, my grandmother cried that she should have been doing that for her boys all those years.

I decided to make my appearance on March 9, 1950, during a history-making blizzard. Nothing could have prepared Mom and Dad for the fourteen-mile trek to the hospital. Dad had to dig out the vehicle, put on double chains, put one-by-sixes down over drifts in the road, and work his way out of a ditch using a team of horses, just to get to the hospital in Gallipolis. I arrived at 11:54 a.m., the oldest grandchild on my mother's side and the youngest grandchild on my father's side.

The entire Lincoln Ridge Community welcomed me, and I was in church within two weeks. I became a churchgoer then and remain so today.

Since I was rarely away from my mother, I soon took my position in her arms as she and Dad sang. To sing in church, therefore, became a regular occurrence. My mother told me that one Sunday morning at age three, I announced that I had a song to sing. Mom attempted to shush me, but the pastor overheard. He told the congregation that a little lady wanted to sing, so he stood me on the front bench, and I boldly sang, "I'll flied away, O Dory; I'll flied away in de mornin'. When I die, halleleu-yur by and by, I'll flied away!"

Growing up as an only child and living a quarter mile from our nearest neighbors, I had a constant companion in my mom. I became aware of that fact around the age of three. Mom taught me to count from one to one hundred and helped me memorize my ABCs by age five. She read to me from Golden Books and from my Bible storybook, played games with me, let me ride on the back of our collie, Lady, and took me with her to do the farm work. In the afternoons, she put me down on a quilt in the living room for a nap. Sometimes I'd wake up, and Mom wouldn't be in the house. I'd go looking for her, hear her talking to someone in the barn, and find her on her knees in a hay mow, pouring out her heart in prayer. I will never forget Mom's prayer altars: the hay mow, the summer porch kitchen, a stump on the hillside, or the corner of the bedroom. I learned early that my mom was a woman of prayer. I also learned that a prayer from her never ascended to heaven without having my dad's and my name spoken in it. That fact became an earth-shattering thought when my mom died, and I realized it would never happen again.

Mom was the family photographer, so we have a very full pictorial history of the Parcell and Stewart families. She had an old Kodak Brownie camera she'd purchased when she worked at the Celanese. She took rolls of pictures at every family, church, and farm event. I have an inheritance of about twenty photo albums. Few pictures would have existed had it not been for Mom and her Brownie.

Mom, like Dad, was a hard worker and adapted well to farm life. When planting or harvesting time came, it was nothing for Mom to cook breakfast and lunch for fifteen to twenty workers and neighbors who were helping Dad. She managed a huge garden, canned the fruit of her labor, killed and dressed chickens, stirred off apple butter, went hunting with Dad, helped with the hog butchering in the fall, and provided a huge breakfast for uncles and cousins who came to the farm to hunt rabbits and squirrels.

She brought good old southern cooking to the Stewart table and was known for her cathead biscuits, fried caramelized sweet potatoes, lemon meringue and coconut cream pies, and pineapple coconut cake. When Dad discovered that frog gigging was a good hunt, she learned to fry frog legs. Frying chicken, pineapple fritters, or doughnuts for Dad's hunts was a regular occurrence. I never heard Mom complain about her lot in life or the work she had to do. She accepted all things as the work of a wife committed to her husband.

My dad was quite a handsome man, and when Dad and Mom traveled around singing, other women would flirt with him. Mom seemed not to notice, or if she did, a gentle smile came upon her face.

When I became old enough to notice, I boldly raised the question with Mom. "Don't you understand that these women are flirting with Dad? Why don't you say or do something?"

Mother smiled a knowing smile. "Honey, sure they are attracted to him. Your dad's a handsome man. But he comes home with me."

I have rarely seen a love as strong as Mom and Dad's. Their marriage matured because of the sacrificial gift of Mom's love for Dad. She had learned it from her parents, and she carried it on into her marriage.

Mom gifted me with a clear shadow of a loving wife and mother—the biblical image of a submissive wife: "Wives, submit yourselves to your own husbands, as it is fit in the Lord" (Colossians 3:18).

CHAPTER 12

He Reached Down His Hand for Me

MOM, LIKE MANY YOUNG WOMEN OF THE DEPRESSION ERA, HAD no formal education beyond high school. Both she and Dad received their education from living life.

My mother learned dependency upon the Lord at quite an early age. God was her fortress. He had "reached down His hand" (the words of a song Mom and Dad often sang) early in her life, and she clung to it faithfully for the rest of her days. Nothing happened in Mom's life that she did not believe God had a purpose for. He was worthy of her trust.

One thing, however, that always troubled Mom was that she had trouble understanding some portions of the Bible. She would comment that she wished she were like Dad and me in being able to explain various Bible verses because we knew the Scriptures so well. I explained that she knew them far better than Dad and I did, for she lived them out before us every single day. I recognized my mother's shadow well, and I longed to walk in it.

Mom taught me lasting principles of God's Word, possibly without even knowing it. It was her manner in dealing with me that made them memorable. For example, I learned that stealing was never profitable. I remember well the events of this lesson.

Because we only had one vehicle, and Mom didn't have a license anyway, Dad would drop us off in downtown Gallipolis every Friday on his way to work. Before we left home, with her finger about two inches from my nose, Mom would give me the behavior talk. She promised that if I behaved myself and didn't touch what did not belong to me, I would receive a treat. Obviously, a long day meant open opportunities for tiredness, peevishness, and misbehavior on my part. We made our doctor and dentist visits, did our window shopping, ate lunch at Gallagher's Drug Store, and finished the day grocery shopping a half block away from Dad's work.

One Friday—I was five at the time—I decided I would like a candy bar, which I spied on a shelf in the candy section of the dime store. Of course, I didn't have any money, but that didn't seem important. The candy was in plain view, and it seemed the only requirement was for me to pick it up.

Mom and I left the store for more errand running, and I opened my candy bar. Mom looked down to find me enjoying the scrumptious treat.

"Where did you get that?" she queried knowingly.

"At the store," I unabashedly replied.

"Did you pay for it?" Her voice grew stern.

"No," I replied guardedly. I suspected I might somehow be in trouble.

"Brenda Jean Stewart."

Hearing all three of my names, I *knew* I was in trouble. "Yes . . ."

"Give me that!"

I think I said, "You mean my candy?"

"Yes!" She spoke adamantly.

I handed the candy bar to her, and we turned back to the dime store. Once inside, Mom asked to see the manager. The clerk was not enough for such a broken law. The manager soon appeared, questioning how he could help.

I depended on Mom to explain the whole thing, but she said, "Go on, Jeanie. Tell the man what you did."

Immediately, I knew what I had to do. Pointing in the direction of the candy section, I confessed. "I took the candy from that shelf."

The manager kindly replied, "That's okay, honey."

My mother immediately cast him a teacher look, even though she wasn't a teacher by profession, and exclaimed, "No, it is not all right! She will pay for it. Jeanie, tell the nice man that you are sorry."

"I'm sorry." I timidly obeyed.

Mom then opened her purse, took out the necessary nickel—yes, a candy bar was a nickel in those days—handed it to the manager, took my hand firmly, and walked me out the door.

I "paid" for the candy bar the next week by pulling weeds from the lettuce bed and gathering eggs, a chore which I detested. I learned "thou shalt not steal" that day. That was my shadow-casting mom.

Somewhere in her young life, my mother learned to esteem others above herself. She desired to make all people comfortable in her home or in any relationship. While she was an attractive woman, she was not vain, and in fact, portrayed an endearing humility. She had no standing in Gallipolitan society or any accumulation of wealth, but she was a favorite among my friends as a homeroom mother, parent chaperone, or part of the fan base at football games.

Of course, at games she would root just as adamantly for the opposing side as she did for our team because the opponents were doing an excellent job too. Forgetting herself and her surroundings, she would stand up and cheer for the opposing team's good play. I would have to grab her coattail and gently pull her down to her seat before our fans openly confronted her. Soon they realized that was just Mom's way; everyone deserved a pat on the back for their efforts.

A thought from *To Kill a Mockingbird* epitomizes my mother's view of others. She knew that you "never really understood a person until you walked around in his or her skin."[1] Mother did not possess a critical spirit, and to that I can readily testify.

When I started junior high, Mom sought work outside the home. She worked for two weeks as an aide at the Gallipolis State Institute. Every evening she would come home crying over the physical and mental conditions of her patients. She soon realized that she could not manage such a job, even though the supervisor begged her to stay. The staff of the hospital recognized Mom's obvious compassion, but the patients' conditions were too heart-wrenching for her to endure.

Since jobs were not readily available to those without a college or two-year-programmed degree, she found a job working at a meat packing plant a short distance from our house. It was demanding work and required her standing on concrete floors for hours at a time. Oftentimes, she would come home late because of some mechanical issue or a late order. But sometimes she would be late because of a mistake someone had made in an order or on the job.

The crew with whom Mom worked were mostly women around her age. One, however, was older and slower than the others. One evening Mom did not arrive home until after seven—a grueling twelve-hour shift. She explained that a fellow worker had messed up an order, and they had to do the work all over again.

Mom said, "I don't understand why Mary can't keep things straight. She's always messing up something."

Both Dad and I looked at her, shocked by this unfamiliar critique. Mom had scarcely uttered the complaint when she burst into tears.

"I shouldn't have said that." She wiped away a tear. "I don't know what Mary goes through. I have never had to walk in her shoes."

That was my mother's shadow—a shadow weeping over cross words against a woman who would never know. Only we and God knew, but Mom made sure her sin was confessed and relationship restored before the night was over.

I learned a patient's trust and patience in my mother's shadow. When she was sixty, Mom spent seventeen weeks in the hospital. The doctors were baffled by her condition. She was hemorrhaging internally, but the source was a mystery. She would receive blood transfusions, and the bleeding would stop only to begin again in a few hours; thus, she was literally bleeding to death.

After numerous tests and scans, the doctors finally determined she had severe diverticulitis. Lesions had formed in ballooning areas of her colon, and her body had formed fistulas to protect itself. These areas were rupturing and causing fever and hemorrhaging. She suffered through four surgeries and a stroke during that time. Through the whole ordeal, Mom rarely complained about the illness, the surgeries, the stroke, her treatment, or anything else. When the nurses came in to draw blood, to set her up for another painful test, or to give her yet another dose of medicine, she would respond with a smile and an offer of one arm or the other. When scores of people came to visit her, they would testify that they had come to encourage her but had gone away encouraged.

I only remember one day in the entire seventeen weeks that Mom had a disagreeable day, but she soon apologized to the hospital staff for her unpleasant, negative responses. The nurses and doctors were amazed at her astonishingly unnecessary confession.

Even when Dad remarked to her doctor that Mom seemed to be a little cranky, he retorted, "Well, what of it? She can be cranky if she wants to be. She's earned it!"

Nevertheless, Mom didn't allow herself to remain cranky. In her mind, her testimony was at stake. She was living out God's Word: "Do all things without murmurings and disputings" (Philippians 2:14).

I saw Jesus and the light of the Holy Spirit in my mom. When Mom and Dad sang in various churches during revival services, Mother's "also" voice was clear and strong, but the look on her face was clearer and stronger. Her face unquestioningly demonstrated that she knew intimately the One about whom she sang.

One song she enjoyed singing was an old southern gospel entitled "It Won't Be Very Long." She and Dad would begin to sing, and Mom's face would take on a light that showed she was in touch with the Holy Spirit. She particularly connected with the lyrics, "When Jesus shall appear, the day is drawing near. Will you be ready then to meet the ransomed throng? Be ready for that day; it won't be very long."

When she reached those words, her right hand would lift and wave in the air, keeping time with the music. Those who were in ear shot would begin to praise the Lord, and inevitably someone would leave his or her seat and walk down the aisle toward the altar. This reaction was not a put-on or a dramatic work-up; it was a genuine connection with her Lord and Savior Jesus Christ through the work of the Holy Spirit. I saw that response over and over in my life. That was my mom's shadow in which I longed to stand.

My mother's role as mom was always unquestionable. Mom was first and foremost my mom. When I needed disciplining, she was not one of those mothers who said, "Wait until your father gets home." If I needed a solid talking to or a spanking—yes, she spanked because that was highly effective and highly biblical—Mom could handle the job. She would also determine if my behavior warranted further support from Dad when he arrived home.

Still, Mom was my best friend. In my pre-driving years, we would often spend Friday and Saturday evenings together, staying up late and watching movies on TV, while Dad was out coon hunting. Mom would pop a huge bowl of popcorn, and we'd drink RCs or Dr Peppers and talk and laugh and talk and laugh.

When time came for me to know the facts of life, I did not ask friends about those things as other girls did. I asked my mom. She never hedged on any of my questions. She told me what I needed to know, truthfully and plainly. I trusted her immensely with every secret and never kept anything from her. She always had time for me, she always had an interest in my activities, and she always lovingly supported me in all that I did. When we were together, we never left each other's company without saying, "I love you." I never doubted for one moment in my life that Jesus Christ loved me because I never doubted for one moment my mom's love for me. The shadow of Christ's love fell upon me through my mom.

I could never have equaled and never will equal the shadow my mother cast upon my life. She accepted everyone just the way they came to her. She never passed judgment upon anyone. She sacrificially served to meet the needs of Dad and me without ever expecting anything in return. She accepted with extraordinary joy anything and everything that life brought her.

These are characteristics of the Lord that I regularly saw modeled in LaVerne Lee Stewart. That is my inheritance, and I know "It Won't Be Very Long" until I am face to face with her in glory.

CHAPTER 13

Code Blue

ON NOVEMBER 9, 1984, WHILE I WAS WITH A GROUP OF STUDENTS at the Wilds Christian Camp in western North Carolina, my dad called to tell me that Mom was in the hospital and was hemorrhaging to death. I left my students in the care of the other sponsors, packed my car, and frankly, sped home to Ohio.

I arrived to find Mom sitting up in bed and smiling cheerfully at many visitors in her room. She hardly looked like a woman on the brink of death, but she was dying internally. The doctors were not immediately able to find the source of the bleeding. Her tests had been inconclusive, and her body protected her from pain and abscesses with tissue walls called fistulas. These areas were rupturing and causing the excessive bleeding and tenderness. The Parcells have a high tolerance to pain, so Mom was only moderately uncomfortable even in her great peril. During that time, we rode a constant roller coaster of experiences with Mom in and out of ICU.

ICU was unusual for Mom because she was highly alert for many of her visits while others around her were in various stages of consciousness. She recognized the dire circumstances of her neighbors more than she realized her own precarious situation. Often patients would code—their heart rates slowing precariously or their pressures dangerously spiking or plummeting. If God did not intervene through the medical staff, these people would step into eternity. Amid the flurry of medical staff and machines, Mom would pray for the person in peril. Nurses and doctors came to Mom's bedside often to thank her for the prayers they knew she was sending to God on their behalf. The staff brought gifts and flowers to Mom when she was on the regular floor in gratefulness for her sweet spirit.

No less of a roller coaster was the waiting room outside the ICU. There the families of ICU patients congregated in the most severe of circumstances, waiting to hear the next word regarding their loved ones. Many camped out, especially if they were far from home.

All of us became somewhat of a family then too. We shared our concerns, food, prayers, and stories to break the tension of the room. I kept my Bible and my journal ever at my side, and the Lord gave me many opportunities to share His Word with those newfound family members. I never cease to be amazed at the opportunities afforded us in times of great trials.

The Edwards family was from Portsmouth, Ohio. The mother was a diabetic, and the severity of the disease had taken her leg. At the time we met them, her body was rebelling with tremendous infection. She was dying.

Mom's bed was directly across from hers in ICU. Mrs. Edwards was on a breathing machine and could only communicate with staff and loved ones with a squeeze of the hand—one squeeze for yes and two squeezes for no in answer to their questions.

Her daughter and I shared the corner of the waiting room, distanced from other groups. We became a support for each other, answering questions when one of us was indisposed and talking well into the wee hours of the mornings. Apart from her mother, her greatest concern was for her brother, who was a soldier in the army and on a mission in Granada. He planned to come home to see his mom, but the family was not sure when he would arrive.

On a Thursday evening, Mrs. Edwards became extremely critical, coding every hour or two. Her daughter had learned that her brother was to arrive by that Friday morning. Each time Mrs. Edwards coded, Mom would pray for her survival, at least until her son could be with his mother.

Mom and Dad's pastor happened to be at the hospital for an emergency room call. At around three in the morning, he stepped into the ICU to check on Mom's condition. Mom was awake ... praying. Mrs. Edwards had coded shortly before, and the personnel had done a miraculous job of ministering to her. When her pastor arrived at her bedside, Mom insisted that he go speak to Mrs. Edwards about her soul. At first, he was resistant, largely because of Mrs. Edwards's difficulty with communicating and the seriousness of her condition. Mom explained the hand-squeeze method of communication and adamantly insisted he talk to Mrs. Edwards. He finally relinquished.

Turning to Mrs. Edwards's bed, he asked if he could talk with her about knowing the Lord Jesus Christ as her Savior. She squeezed his hand once for yes. He asked if she had been born again by the power of His Word. She squeezed twice for no. He asked if she would like to know about Jesus. One squeeze. He began relaying the gospel message. Did she understand she was a sinner? One squeeze. He explained that the wages of her sin were death, but the gift of God was eternal life. Did she understand? One squeeze. He explained how Jesus sacrificially died on the cross for the sins of the whole world. Did she understand that Christ died for her sins? One squeeze. The pastor gave the full plan of salvation.

Then he asked the ultimate question: "Are you ready to ask Jesus to be your Savior?"

One squeeze. He asked to lead her in the sinner's prayer, and right there, Mrs. Edwards accepted Jesus and recognized that she was a cherished child of God. Mother rejoiced with tears of joy. Soon after, somewhere around four in the morning, Mrs. Edwards coded again. The staff worked with her, and she was still with them and still responsive. Her son was to arrive early that morning. He arrived in the waiting room at 4:50 a.m., and he and his sister quickly headed to the ICU to see their mom. My mom prayed through the whole visit that Mrs. Edwards would be able to hear her son and that they would be able to communicate their love for each other. God answered her pleas. Overwhelmed with grief, her son and daughter left the unit, and then Mrs. Edwards coded for the final time. Mrs. Edwards went home to be with the Lord at 5:20 a.m.

In the book of Esther, the Bible describes Esther as a selected queen for "such a time as this." I can believe that God allowed my mother to be in the ICU for such a time so that Mrs. Edwards could know her Savior. Only eternity will tell, but I know the pastor was convinced as he told us of his experience with Mom in the ICU. He declared that he would not have even approached Mrs. Edwards had Mom not insisted.

Mom came through those seventeen weeks by the grace of God. Her faith would be further tested years later by my dad's sudden and equally puzzling illness.

In April 1993, my dad began to experience constant nausea. Nothing over the next four months provided adequate sustenance for him. Among the other heart-wrenching symptoms were constant hiccups that tormented him day and night. After countless tests at the local hospital, his doctors sent him to Ohio State University (OSU) Hospital. I followed the ambulance as it sped through the mass of highways in Columbus, knowing somehow that Mom needed to be able to see her husband, even encased in an emergency vehicle.

When we arrived at the hospital, the doctors began their examinations and tests. His doctors told us that they could find nothing conclusive in their tests either. Dad did not have cancer, but his liver had become enlarged, and his fever was mounting. We had arrived at OSU on Thursday, and Dad was in the ICU by Saturday. He was critical and semiconscious by Sunday. The team of doctors had contacted the Atlanta CDC, who were sending a team of specialists on Tuesday. Monday morning, Dad was nonresponsive, but we hung on to the idea of the team from Atlanta being the miracle that God would wrought for Dad.

During Dad's time at OSU, family and friends came to visit. One steadfast friend was there for us from the start. His name was Arthur Jeffers—he preferred Jeff—one of Dad's coon hunting buddies whom he had witnessed to about the Lord. I had been able to present the gospel to his wife Judy, and she had become a Christian as well. We were staying with them in their Columbus home, although Mom and I were actually living at the hospital round the clock. Jeff would become a regular fixture in the waiting rooms with us.

On Monday afternoon, a young man came into the ICU waiting room. He was so distraught that he literally tried to climb the walls. He yo-yoed between cursing and crying out in anguish. I could tell by Jeff's nervous fidgeting that he wanted to tell him to shut up when he cursed, since he was using such language in the presence of what Jeff believed to be dear Christian ladies. At least at that point, Jeff refrained from an outward demonstration of his internal seething.

After some time, the young man finally came over to where Mom, Jeff, and I were sitting and took a seat across from us. A nurse soon came out to tell us that Dad's bed had been tilted again so that his blood pressure would rise to keep his heart functioning. This report came at regular intervals in the medical team's valiant effort to keep Dad alive until the Atlanta team of doctors could see him.

Intervening in our conversation, the young man asked some blunt questions. The conversation became a lesson in patience for Jeff and an open invitation to share the gospel for us.

"Who is she talking about?" the young man asked.

I answered, "My dad."

"What's happening?"

I explained the measures that the medical team were taking.

"Is he dying?" he boldly questioned. I saw Jeff's face turn a bright red. Jeff often had difficulty with his anger; Dad knew not to discuss politics or the poor performance of Jeff's coon dogs with him for fear of an explosion. Now, with red face and pulsing temple, he obviously believed this young man's tone needed addressing.

"Yes," I said.

With an even more challenging tone, the man asked, "Don't you care?"

Jeff's body stiffened. His hands were drawn into fists, and he was poised to strike. I thought he would launch off the couch at any moment to clock the young offender.

Resting my hand on his shoulder, I responded to Jeff's actions. "It's all right, Jeff. I can see why he would ask such a question."

I recognized that only the Christian can rest in the providential care of God for their loved ones; to others, that inexplicable peace is difficult to comprehend. Jeff sat back but not without his fists being ready and able. God, however, was preparing Jeff to receive a lesson in patience and endurance largely from my mother.

Mom spoke next. Though I don't remember her exact words, they were something like this: "Clarence, my husband, is in the hands of the

Lord. We do care, but we know that Clarence is going to a far better place than this old, sinful earth. We are praying for a miracle, but our God is in control, and we are resting in that fact." She gave him a gentle smile. "Do you have someone in the ICU?" Mom tenderly questioned.

"My fiancée!" he explained in a loud voice, interspersed with wailing. "They won't tell me what is happening!"

He went on. "I was driving down the Olentangy when this guy comes over into my lane. I laid on my horn and swerved to miss him. I lost control of the car. The next thing I knew, we had hit this tree. My sister and I in the front were okay, but my fiancée was in the back. The whole side of the car was caved in. She was so bloody and broken."

We would later learn that the doctors were treating her for severe brain injury.

Confessing that he had overcompensated for the swerve to miss the vehicle, he moaned. "It's my fault!"

His story was interrupted by the nurse's coming to tell us that Dad's bed had been lowered. We thanked her kindly and continued to talk with the young man.

Watching our reaction, the young man asked, "How can you do that? How can you sit there and hear what they are saying and not be out of your minds?"

If memory serves me correctly, Jeff, moving to the edge of his seat, responded with, "Now look here. You have no right to question . . ."

"Jeff." Again, I assured him. "It's okay. We can handle his questions. It's all right."

Jeff sat back but continued to rub one fist into his other opened hand.

"We are grieved to lose Dad," I replied, "but at this moment we are more concerned about you."

Jeff's jaw dropped with that statement. I knew then that not only was God about to do a work in this young man, but also Jeff was about to see and hear the Holy Spirit in action.

"How can you help me?" He groaned with his head in his hands. "No one can help me!"

Seeing that God had opened a door, Mom walked through it first. Over the next hour, we presented the gospel to this man who saw no hope. I honestly cannot tell you what we said, in what order we presented God's Word, or how we said it. I know we began with talking of the love of God for this man's fiancée and for him. I recall using Romans 5:8, but we were so in tune with the Holy Spirit that I cannot tell anyone what we said from then on. I know we later marveled at the words of Scripture that poured from our lips—Scriptures that we had not spoken for some time.

I would love to say that right there in the waiting room the young man came to know the Lord as his own personal Savior. He did not. The doctors came to tell him his fiancée was in her unit and that he could go see her. We never saw him again, and we never knew what happened to him or his fiancée.

"We will be praying for you and your fiancée," Mom said as the man left the room. We prayed right then. I learned early on from my pastor's wife to always pray immediately after a promise of prayer so that I would not lie to the person or to the Holy Spirit.

When my uncle Arthur and aunt Helen came into the waiting room to visit after that encounter, it was not Mom or me who told of our experience—it was our friend Jeff.

"I couldn't believe the way that guy spoke to LaVerne and Jeanie. He made me mad, and I was ready to show him the door. But then they began to share verses with him. They didn't use their Bibles, but they sure did quote some powerful words. I wish I knew the Bible like that!" Jeff shared.

"Jeff, I don't know the Bible that well to quote it from memory," Mom said. "Those words came from what I had read, and the Holy Spirit used them to speak to that boy, not me."

I added, "Jeff, I don't even remember what we said. I couldn't repeat it now if I tried. I can only marvel that the Holy Spirit showed up and preached His Word."

"Well," Jeff said, "I know I learned not to fly off the handle. I could have ruined it all today. I am thankful that I was able to be here to hear what went on."

Jeff heard the Holy Spirit give His word of salvation to a man in deep spiritual need. Jeff learned that day, especially from Mom, the patience to accept rebuke from a lost someone in order to gain an opportunity to share the gospel. He also clearly saw that we had only been the mouthpieces for the Holy Spirit.

The next morning, shortly after eleven, we said goodbye to my dad after assuring him that he had been a wonderful husband and father and that he had been an example of the Lord Jesus Christ. We genuinely believed that Dad heard our loving words as he stepped out into eternity with Jesus.

In the sanctuary room of OSU Hospital, friends, doctors, and relatives had gathered with us. We were both crying and praising God for a life well lived before us. How could we deny God's perfect healing for my dad that day? We celebrated his life in that little room. Jeff was there with us and witnessed the calm assurance that God had welcomed home another of His children. As we talked through what was to come next, my mom confidently and passionately spoke the words of a song she and Dad would often sing: "He Reached Down His Hand for Me."

Jeff exclaimed afterward, "I never knew that a person could rejoice over someone's dying until today. Praise God! I know Clarence is home with Jesus."

Dad died in September of 1993. Although Mom experienced this great loss, she retained that joy in serving Jesus by being an encourager to those around her. She continued to worship in the little country church home that she and Dad had found, until her body began to betray her.

In 1999, Mom and I bought a little cottage in St. Albans, West Virginia. Our neighbors and church members embraced her warmth and gentle spirit. She would merely sit on the porch swing and folks would stop by to visit or leave vegetables on the porch steps for her to find. She delighted in their company. We traveled together to lighthouses and covered bridges and would have a picnic lunch on the James River after a morning of sightseeing.

She would remark at each new adventure, "Your father would have loved this."

In 2004, Mom went home to be with the Lord on a glorious Sunday morning. Her means of death was an answer to prayer we had been praying for more than a year: that whoever left this life first—it was not assured that Mom would go to heaven before me—would do so at home, would not be alone, and would go in peace. God honored that prayer in miraculous ways.

A dear friend, Abby, was visiting with us. We were getting ready for church before Abby was to fly home that afternoon.

From Mom's bedroom across the hall, I heard her say, "Well, I almost fell."

I knew she had been sitting on the edge of her bed putting on her shoes.

I walked quickly to her room in time to hear her say, "Oh . . ." in a wondrous tone.

I arrived at her bedside as she pitched forward. I caught her in my arms on the way down. She died there with that same gentle, assured smile I had always known.

On Mom and Dad's gravestone is the epithet: "He Reached Down His Hand for Me." Even in death, their relationship with God continues to resonate as people walk by that gravesite and comment on the message engraved there. I have every assurance that both Mom and Dad are with the Lord.

Because of their faith and relationship with Him, I have been privileged to walk in their shadows. Because of my mom, I have the steadfast assurance that I accepted the invitation and opened my heart's door to Christ. Because of His finished work, I know that I have an inheritance in heaven awaiting me.

I know determinedly that with Jesus Christ we only walk "through the valley of the shadow of death," for heaven waits on the other side.

CHAPTER 14

A Tribute

by Clarence A. Stewart

I WISH YOU COULD HAVE KNOWN UNCLE ELI. BETTER STILL, I WISH everyone could have had an Uncle Eli.

Who in the world was Uncle Eli? Actually, he was my great-uncle. But he was "Uncle" to everyone who knew him, young and old alike. What made Uncle Eli so special? I do not really know. I do know that he has been gone for around thirty-five years, and I still have fond memories of him and think of him often. I find myself wondering just what made him the most unforgettable character I have ever met.

He was rather tall of stature—I would say about six foot three or four—rather large and muscular but with not one ounce of fat . . . all lean. He was as straight as a Kentucky colonel and in a certain way sort of reminded me of one. However, he was never in the military. He usually wore a black hat—summer or winter.

I recall his visits to our home when I was a child as though they were yesterday. I was always glad to see him come and sorry to see him leave. He lived about twenty miles from us and thought nothing of walking to our house on a Saturday and then walking back home on Sunday. He had a certain spring in his heel and a certain gleam in his eye that a person just could not forget.

My mother sometimes would look out the window and see him coming half a mile down the road and say, "Yonder comes Uncle Eli; I would know that walk anywhere."

He usually would bring his accordion with him, and I loved to hear him play.

One time he came, and when he was ready to leave, he said, "You like that so well, I'm going to leave it with you, and if you can play it when I come again, I am going to give it to you."

Needless to say, I learned to play it, and he gave it to me.

Uncle Eli never married. Why? I don't know. He always lived alone and made his living digging coal. Those were the days when coal was mined by hand and pushed out of the mine in a coal buggy, which held twelve and a half bushels or a half ton.

Perhaps you don't see anything unusual so far. Well, I was about to get to that. He was one of the few people I have met in my life who had no selfish motives whatsoever. He loved kids, and that is where he spent what money he made: on kids. He would gather all the kids together at an ice cream social or pie supper and buy for every one of them. He would go home broke but happy. Those kids grew up loving him; all of them called him Uncle Eli. To be known that way seemed to be all he wanted out of life.

After automobiles came along and we had a little better way of traveling, my mom sometimes would fry chicken and fix a picnic basket. We would go get him and take him with us to a favorite spot for lunch. Every house we passed on the way, if the kids happened to be outside playing, they would all wave at him and yell, "Hi, Uncle Eli."

Uncle Eli loved to sing and had a rich, deep bass voice. Whenever his name was mentioned around the adults, they would always say, "I remember Uncle Eli. I sure loved to hear him sing. Nobody could sing like him."

Since I've gotten older and have met so many people in life, it seems that most of us have a good side and one that is not so good. If this old man had a bad side, he sure kept it well-concealed because I never, ever saw it. Makes me wonder if he had a secret that most of us haven't discovered. He never seemed to run low on something to give, and whatever he gave, there was always a gift of love thrown in for good measure.

He lived to be ninety-six, and I cannot remember his being sick a day in his life.

Jeanie's Note: Uncle Eli's legacy to my father was love and a generous spirit. Dad regularly shared his memories of his uncle.

Dad, Mom, and I searched southern Lawrence County, Ohio, for his gravesite. When we finally found it, Dad had a stone erected with the word "Uncle" placed on the top of it. The stonecutter knew the name well, as did most of the older generation who lived in that area.

When we would take flowers at decoration time, several bouquets would already be present on the grave. Clearly, he meant much to his community, as he did to my family. I never knew him, but somehow I could imagine him standing next to me whenever my father sang.

I, too, had a tradition from Uncle Eli.

CHAPTER 15

Ship Ahoy!

MY FATHER CAST A LENGTHY SHADOW. HE WAS SIX THREE AND had, according to the doctor who once removed a sizable wood splinter from his palm, "the largest hands I have ever seen."

Dad, like his mother, was a proud man. Proud of his stature, his wife, and his country. Dad was a member of the Greatest Generation and was a staff sergeant in the United States Army Air Corps during World War II. He was proud of his daughter as well, but for whatever reason, he told others about that pride, but he failed to tell me. At times, our relationship was tenuous. At other times, it seemed ideal. Dad was my rock and my anchor through the storms of life and, sadly, through the storms of his displeasure.

As a child, his intelligence extended beyond his teachers. His high school French teacher often asked Dad to translate, because Dad could speak the language so much more fluently than the teacher. He also was fascinated by geometry. He would use it later in life to construct houses and staircases and to clear a furnace room of its coal contents.

I believe Dad would have been a wonderful teacher, but the Great Depression robbed him of any opportunity to be what he wanted. Many during that era had only an eighth-grade education, but at least Dad stayed in school until after his sophomore year. He then withdrew to help provide for his family's survival during those tough times. He never returned to a formal education. Life was his teacher for the rest of his days.

He became a soldier, bread truck driver, farmer, carpenter, floor sander (his main occupation), and finally a custodial maintenance man in an elementary school. Was he a wealthy man? A learned man with a degree after his name? A man admired for his station in life? No. Was he highly revered? Yes.

Dad was known over all of Gallia County and much of the state of Ohio for his floor sanding craftsmanship and for his honesty. Dad worked hard, lifting the two-hundred-fifty-pound floor sanding machine in and out of his truck and up and down stairs for thirty-three years. Bent over for so many years and finishing floors with an edger eventually wore out the disks in his back. The wide girth that he used to apply the finish to the floors astounded those who watched. He could coat a floor quicker and more smoothly than anyone I ever knew. The work on the farm had been no less demanding, but Dad took immense pride in a hard day's work and his "wet-shirt" mentality.

Dad would tell the truth even if it "took the hide off," as he said. That fact tarnished our relationship for life. He was not reticent in sharing the truth of my inadequacies, and we had many heart-to-heart talks about what I needed to do to improve myself. I understood in my head that Dad was doing his best to help me and these talks were the only way he knew how to help, but I felt in my heart the wounds of his honest words!

In spite of those wounds, from my father's example, I admit I learned the importance of telling the truth.

During my third-grade year, Dad decided that his business was too much to maintain while still trying to manage a farm, so we moved and left our rural home. I left the farm life I knew for the "big city" of Gallipolis.

I met a whole new group of people who were foreign to me. They knew things I did not know. I was frightened that they would never accept me into their circle of friends, so I played on the playground alone many days until I became brave enough to step into their circles. I learned quickly that I needed a life that matched theirs; I did not have one, so I made one up.

In my early days, I had a throng of imaginary playmates, so having an imaginary life was not so difficult. My classmates drew closer to me when I told my made-up stories. I experimented with lying and exaggerating until it finally caught up with me in my seventh-grade year. I, along with some other equally creative students, had invented some quite historical backgrounds for ourselves.

My dad's emphasis on truth-telling caught up with me when our history teacher shared those stories with parents at a parent-teacher meeting. I had a day of reckoning with my parents when we arrived home. Truth was truth even if it took the hide off, or if it meant that I would have to admit publicly that I was not a descendant of James Stewart of Scotland and hadn't visited Scotland when I was a young child. The truth came close to taking my hide off. I learned then that Dad meant what he said about honesty. I rarely received a spanking from my father; his hands were so large and he was so strong that he feared he would really hurt me. This time, however, he gave me the spanking I deserved. He didn't beat me or inflict bodily harm; he merely applied the hand of his teaching to the seat of my learning.

In a psych class in college, I learned that alcoholics, though cured, would always be alcoholics, a result of their addiction. I began to understand and apply that information to form a biblical view of my temptations: I am and always will be a liar . . . forgiven, just as I am, and always a sinner saved by grace. But the inherited penchant for truth telling became a shadow I continue to walk within.

Dad's business was honest, his dealing with people was honest, and his love was honest. That character trait made him well-known among business leaders in the community. And though I agreed with my father's words, I did not agree with his method. However, his parents had raised him in that same honesty, and he believed that he was showing his love by his brusque truth telling.

Daddy took pride in his deep, resounding voice. Mom and Dad's duet singing reminded me of the lyrics of an old country song: "Daddy sang bass, Momma sang tenor." Their singing together was among the greatest church memories I have. Dad's bass voice had a rich sound, deeper and lower than most basses could go. He delighted in singing and would do so at every opportunity. He and my mom sang in little country churches all over southeastern Ohio and parts of West Virginia. Being an only child and in the constant charge of my mother, I have early and vivid memories of those occasions. Again, only heaven will tell of the many people their singing impacted and the many who came to a church's altar when they would sing in a revival.

On occasion, someone in the crowd would ask Dad to sing "The Old Ship of Zion (Ship Ahoy),"[2] which was one of his favorite songs. The lyrics of the song go like this:

> I was drifting away on life's pitiless sea,
> And the angry waves threatened my ruin to be,
> When away at my side, there I dimly descried,
> A stately old vessel, and loudly I cried:
> "Ship ahoy! Ship ahoy!"
> And loudly I cried: "Ship ahoy!"
>
> 'Twas the "old ship of Zion," thus sailing along,
> All aboard her seemed joyous, I heard their sweet song;
> And the Captain's kind ear, ever ready to hear,
> Caught my wail of distress, as I cried out in fear:
> "Ship ahoy! Ship ahoy!"
> As I cried out in fear: "Ship ahoy!"
>
> The good Captain commanded a boat to be low'red,
> *And with tender compassion He took me on board;*
> *And I'm happy today, all my sins washed away*
> *In the blood of my Savior, and now I can say*:
> "Bless the Lord! Bless the Lord!"
> From my soul I can say: "Bless the Lord!"
>
> O soul, sinking down 'neath sin's merciless wave,
> The strong arm of our Captain is mighty to save;
> Then trust Him today, no longer delay,
> Board the old ship of Zion, and shout on your way:
> "Jesus saves! Jesus saves!"

Dad's love of that song was ironic to me because for years Dad and I debated the security of salvation. He believed that the Baptist idea of security of the believer gave license to live any way the saved chose, since they were, as the song said, "safe and secure" from hell. In addition, his upbringing had taught him that works were necessary for salvation, and people could lose their salvation if their lifestyle did not match their testimony. I, from my Baptist teaching (Mom and Dad allowed me to attend First Baptist because of the youth activities) and my own Bible reading, believed that once in grace, always in grace.

When I was twenty-two, Dad came home from work one day praising the Lord. He had been listening to a radio broadcast featuring the Scripture, "Let down your net for a draught" (Luke 5:1–11). Dad had read those verses more times than I, I am sure, but that day's radio message had opened a new idea: let down your net.

He said, "I have always cast my net with my own efforts instead of letting down my net and allowing the Lord to do the work instead of doing the work myself. I understand what you have been saying all along."

We had a new understanding between us that day, and we grew closer, but he continued to wound me time and time again with his harsh words when he tried to help me understand the truth about myself. Although I truly know Dad knew the Lord Jesus Christ as his Savior, I know on that day, he anchored his soul in the truth of the Word. It is the finished work of Jesus Christ alone that secures our salvation, not the work we do. As "The Old Ship of Zion" says, "Jesus saves! Jesus saves!" God said it; that settles it!

After that day, Dad began doing something that I am so thankful for today. He secured a package of yellow tablets, a pack of pencils, and the dictionary I had given him for his birthday. Armed with all the tools he needed, he began to write.

The next four chapters are Dad's story and his heirlooms to me, in his own words.

I include a personal note to describe how he left me that inheritance, among so many other things!

CHAPTER 16

My Creed

by Clarence A. Stewart

I HEREBY EXPRESS MY BELIEFS AS TO WHAT THE BIBLE TEACHES:

I believe in the sovereignty of God.

I believe in the holiness of God.

I believe in the Trinity: Father, Son, and Holy Ghost.

I believe in the virgin birth of Jesus Christ.

I believe that He was born for a specific purpose: to seek and to save that which was lost.

He (God) had to be robed in human flesh in order to become a mediator between a Holy God and sinful mankind.

I believe He (Jesus) fulfilled every jot and tittle of the holy Law of God.

I believe it pleased the Father to bruise Him.

I believe in two advents.

I believe He came at His first advent as a suffering servant, a sacrificial Lamb.

I believe He came not to be ministered unto but to minister.

I believe He will come again in power and great glory as King of Kings and Lord of Lords.

I believe He came first in mercy, the next time in judgment.

I believe this will be a literal return.

I believe the treasure hid in the field to be Israel.

I believe the "pearl of great price" to be the church through salvation.

I believe salvation must be received, not achieved.

89

I believe that salvation is by grace plus nothing.

I believe salvation is by faith (which is also a gift of God) in the finished work of Calvary and the bodily resurrection of Christ.

I believe His promise in which He said, "Because I live, you can."

I believe salvation to mean deliverance from the power and penalty of sin.

I believe sin is a condition, not an act.

I believe we are delivered from a state of condemnation to a state of adoption whereby we cry, "Abba, Father."

I don't believe there can be real conversion aside from Holy Ghost conversion.

I don't believe that it is according to man's free will. By that, I mean I don't believe man can make his will sensitive to the gospel, as clearly seen in the following Scriptures:

> "Which were born, not of blood, nor of the will of the flesh, nor of the will of man, but of God." (John 1:13)

> "Because the carnal mind is enmity against God: for it is not subject to the law of God, neither indeed can be." (Romans 8:7)

> "Moreover whom he did predestinate, them he also called: and whom he called, them he also justified: and whom he justified, them he also glorified." (Romans 8:30)

I believe salvation is eternal.

I believe it is of the Lord, not man.

I don't believe that free grace is in any way a license to sin (although it may be abused by those who don't understand it). On the contrary, I believe it to be the only inspiration for godly living.

I also believe it is the only remedy from sin.

I believe that if we are not chastened of the Lord, then we are bastards and not sons.

I believe there is a sin unto death.

If we refuse chastening, God has a perfect right to take natural life.

I believe it is Christ's righteousness imputed to our account that makes it acceptable in the beloved, and we are complete in Him.

I believe that we are to be His ambassadors while in this world.

I believe we are kept by the power of God through faith to an inheritance which is incorruptible, and fadeth not away reserved in heaven (1 Peter 1).

I believe premillennialism—the rapture of the church prior to the great tribulation.

I believe the judgment seat of Christ is for believers (works will be tried to see of what sort we are) and the great white throne judgment at least a thousand years later for the unsaved.

I believe that the stone that the builders rejected is Christ.

If we fall on that stone for mercy, then it will grind us to powder.

Jeanie's note: My father did not have a formal education, let alone a seminary one. These beliefs he affirmed solely from God's Word. He believed in the inheritance that comes from knowing the Lord, Jesus Christ, as Savior.

I found this writing after my father passed away, yet I knew his beliefs from the life that he lived, the discussions he had with others and me, and the things he taught me personally.

His creed is my creed as well: one of the many things he bequeathed to me.

CHAPTER 17

Real Revival

by Clarence A. Stewart

FOR THE PAST TWO NIGHTS, WE HAVE BEEN PRIVILEGED TO LISTEN to some good, sound Bible preaching in a revival service. As I ponder the efforts that are put forth to try to revive the professed church, many thoughts go through my mind.

First, I find myself wondering why we don't see real revival anymore. I have been privileged to visit prayer rooms in several churches where there were revival efforts being put forth. Mostly the prayer requests are for some who are sick in body or for unsaved people. I'm not being critical. These things are honorable and right, but I get the notion that we may have our priorities slightly out of focus. We seem to have the attitude that the revival is for the unsaved. Not so. You just can't revive a dead person; he needs to have had lived in order to be brought to life.

I can't remember when I've heard a pastor or a layman say, "Pray for me that I may be able to have the power of God on my life that I might be able to go where the lost man is and be able to bind up his wounds, pour in some oil and wine, and take him to a place of safety."

Some time ago, I was lying on my bed wondering why we don't see real revival. This thought came to me almost immediately; we don't want it! We like our lives just the way they are. Surely, God can send revival if we desire it.

It has been my conviction for a long time that we pray because of our needs. If we find ourselves comfortable, we have problems sensing a need in our lives. We are apt to pray for God's blessings when we already are head over heels in blessings. We will notice by studying Old Testament Scriptures that the prophets of old didn't pray for God to bless His people when they had been disobedient. On the contrary, they usually prayed for God to get the people's attention, no matter what it took.

Second, many of my convictions do not seem to correspond with what we hear preached nowadays, and I find myself wondering if I am just not up with the times. We often see people making decisions. I suppose when we get right down to basic facts, there is a decision to be made, but I wonder what ever happened to Holy Spirit conviction. I find myself wondering if there can be any real conversion aside from Holy Spirit conviction. Have we found by man's wisdom a way that we are attempting to perform a work in the power of the flesh, that is the work of the Holy Spirit that He must do? I base this assumption on the Scripture that says, "No man can come to me, except the Father which hath sent me draw him" (John 6:44).

Some time ago, I was reading in the book of Daniel where Belshazzar made a great feast and commanded to bring the vessels of gold and silver out of the temple of God, and they drank wine and praised the gods of gold, of silver, of brass, of iron, of wood, and of stone. Then there came a finger writing on the wall, which caused great fear to come upon him.

As we think back on this occasion, we tend to think this was just horrible, but then as I ponder these things, I find myself wondering just what kind of God we really worship. Do we worship the true and living God who made us? Or do we worship the one that we make who warms our bodies, fills our stomachs, and makes us feel good?

I admit this is a sobering thought, but Scripture does warn us that our bodies are the temple of the Holy Ghost, and if any man defiles the temple, him will God destroy. As I write this, I must confess that I find it difficult to invite the Holy Spirit to check me out and put His finger on the things in my own life that are not pleasing to Him. I find it much easier to point Him to someone else's sin.

I wonder just what would happen in revival if we were to be honest with God. If we could bring ourselves to the place where we could be honest with God, I think we could then be honest with each other. It is beyond my reasoning why we insist on pretending, but pretend we will. We just must try to impress someone. I doubt if God is impressed by our pretense. We act as though God operates on the same principles as the laws of the land. If we break the law of the land and don't get caught, then we think no one needs know about it. God just doesn't operate that way.

I don't know if there is a specific formula for revival. First, as I said before, I feel we need to desire to see revival. And as old fashioned as it might sound, I believe real revival comes through a brokenhearted church—a church that has a burden for the unsaved. It has been many years since I've been in a service where I sensed the presence of the Holy Spirit to the degree that conviction hovered over the congregation like a cloud.

Some time ago, I got to wondering why men like Dwight Moody had such great success back in their day, so I bought some of his books. I was curious to see what messages he preached that reached the hearts of so many people.

Strange as it might seem, his message differed very little from what the called man of God preaches today. After all, there is only one message in Scripture for salvation in any age. I was much interested in the way he prayed. It seemed that he expected God to respond to his requests and had little or no doubt that He would. I would have to believe, too, that the church perhaps responded to the preaching back in those days better than we do now.

Jeanie's note: Dad has been with the Lord since 1993. Many years have passed, but the concerns have not dissipated. Do we see real revival today? Do we Christians even see the need for revival, or are we comfortable the way things are? Do we earnestly pray for revival? Have we seen Holy-Spirit-sent conviction? More importantly, would we know it if we saw it?

I may have inherited the same concerns as my father. Are they your concerns as well? Are your children's lives at stake in this present age? Do we yearn to see them saved, renewed in the Spirit, and living out Christ in their lives?

Do we really *want* revival?

CHAPTER 18

The Victorious Christian

by Clarence A. Stewart

IT SHOULD, I SUPPOSE, BE THE DESIRE OF EVERY BORN-AGAIN Christian to be victorious. However, it seems to me, especially in this day in which we live (written in 1992), that many Christians, if they would be honest, would have to admit that they live defeated lives a good portion of the time. So the question would seem to be, is this victorious life so elusive that regardless of how hard we try to find it, somehow it eludes us?

During my life, with most of the preaching that I have listened to along this line, I have interpreted it to be of a scolding nature. To put it more simply, the pastor has decided he can whip his people into shape so they can straighten up and fly right. Sad to say, but truthfully, I haven't seen this accomplished very much.

It would seem that after so long a time, if a minister's message isn't getting the job done, he should be able to see it and to seek God's way. I'm not saying that he is to compromise his convictions, and I realize that a minister has to be stern at times, but if by being stern, he gets hold of the wrong spirit, he is not going to help anyone. Contrarily, he is likely to do much damage.

What then is the solution to this problem? Just what is the answer to this situation? Do I knock myself out trying to improve my own self-image? Do I get the notion that if I do certain things, God will look favorably on me? Do I make bargains with God that if He will do certain things for me, then I will do certain things for Him? What about the times when I ask for sunshine, and He sends rain?

When my wife was critically ill several years ago and needed several units of blood, one of our friend's two teenage boys each gave a unit of blood and dedicated it to her. This type of gift doesn't require payment. In fact, there is no way that we can pay for a gift of love.

It has been my observation that we insist on trying to pay God back for giving His Son for us. We say because You have been so good to me, I just want to pay You back so we will be even. It doesn't seem to dawn on us that after we have done our absolute best, then the Bible says we are still unprofitable servants.

Lest we forget, I am still talking about becoming victorious Christians.

I'd like to relate a story that I heard an old preacher tell some years back. He said he had never been a churchgoer before he became a Christian. Then, his first impression of the pastor's sermon was that church was the place where the pastor told his listeners how mean they were.

On Wednesday nights, they had what they called a testimony meeting. This preacher, as a young man, decided that church is where people tell the pastor how good they are, and vice versa. Since the pastor insisted that self-surrender was the answer, the young man would go back to the altar and surrender. He would then go to this secret prayer closet and surrender.

The pastor had said, "Just let God run your life."

That sounded good, so the young man added, "That's it. Here, God, You run my life."

The pastor also said, "Empty yourself and let God fill your cup."

So the young man tried that. He would hold up his cup and say, "Here, Lord, fill my cup." He would look in his cup, and it would be dry as dust.

His next endeavor followed his pastor's instruction to, "Crucify the flesh!"

The young man thought that sure sounded good. There was no question but what the flesh was the problem. But he wondered, how do you do it? He finally decided he was just a weak person, and he would do his best and *hope* for the best. Surely, God did not expect more than that.

There is quite a lesson here if we can grasp it. Yes, God does require more than our best, but what He requires, He furnishes. You can easily see that all these things which the old preacher had tried as a young believer were an attempt to improve on the flesh, which is an impossibility. If we are to be perfectly honest, we have all been guilty of this very thing.

Bear in mind that the man who told this story had been a minister for many years. If these things didn't work for *him,* why do *we* insist on trying this same route? Is there some kind of mysterious solution to the struggles we face?

How about the two men who went to the temple to pray? How often have we been guilty of trying to present our good works to God? We say, "God, didn't You notice how faithful I've been? Didn't You see how much I put in the offering plate? You haven't forgotten that truck load of clothing I took to the city mission, have You?"

Perhaps, you are not guilty of these thoughts, but because of the fact that I have been, I would have to think you have been too.

Am I able to say, "If you want to be a victorious Christian, here is the formula?"

I'm afraid not. I sure wish I could.

Some things I have learned, however. We do desire to bring God down to our level. He tells us that His thoughts are not our thoughts. His ways are not our ways. In other words, God is not who we think He is. He is who He *says* He is. The only way we can expect God to deal with us is according to His mercy.

What I'm trying to point out is that God owes us nothing. We don't send God a bill for what He owes us, for things we have done for Him. If I am to be victorious, I need Him to do something for me. This is contrary to much of the preaching we listen to today. We insist on trying to merit His favor. If we do, then we are not living the Christian life by grace but by indebtedness.

"This is the victory that overcometh the world, even our faith" (1 John 5:4). The answer to many of our struggles is that our faith must work by love. As the teenagers gave blood for my wife because of love, and as I pointed out, that kind of gift can't be paid for and must be accepted as such. By the same token, our redemption must be accepted the same way. Regularly living in this manner is living victoriously.

Jeanie's note: I have worked in education for almost fifty years. The shifts in culture are obvious, but the ironic thing is that students still need the same things. They need someone to set boundaries for their protection; they need someone to love them; they need someone to challenge them to do their best; and they need us to show forth Christ in all that we do.

The victorious Christian is one who believes the Word with all his heart, soul, mind, and strength. He is not perfect, but he seeks to live out that intimate, personal relationship with Christ every single day. I came to this conclusion from years of experience and the wisdom bequeathed to me by my father.

CHAPTER 19

God's Handiwork

DAD LOVED THE OUTDOORS. HE WAS A HUNTER AND OFTENTIMES a fisherman. Dad knew that God did not dwell in nature, but He did believe that God's design in nature was there for many purposes: to show forth His glory, to show us His power, and to teach us valuable life lessons. These life lessons were the things I fondly remember.

Dad taught me how to know my way around the woods. For instance, moss grows on the north side of a tree.

He showed me how to dress game and taught me anatomy while going through the process.

He taught me how to measure and double measure before cutting wood.

He taught me to look at the design in the wood and read God's fingerprint in its design. He explained that dogwood reflected the story of the crucifixion: the blossoms have three pierced petals with a stain of "blood" around each piercing and a "crown of thorns" in the middle.

He taught me to look at the stars and appreciate the magnitude of God.

Often his lessons would begin with the words, "Look. What do you see?"

I would look in the direction of his pointing, focus more closely, and draw a dumbfounded conclusion: *I don't have a clue what he is seeing, but I know a lesson is coming.*

One quiet summer day, we were sitting on the side porch of our farm-house. He was looking at the maple tree in the side yard.

Suddenly, the question came. "What do you see?"

I looked carefully and was sure I had the answer he was prodding me for. "There are empty locust shells hanging in the bark of the tree."

"No, that's not it," he said.

I searched with all my might, but I could not see anything astounding. "Nothing, Dad. I don't see anything but a tree."

"Look again," he replied.

I did as I was told. I looked doggedly, completely focused on the tree. Still nothing. "I still don't see anything, Dad."

"Look at the roots of the tree."

I eyed them carefully and somewhat begrudgingly. The roots were thick on the far side of the tree, sticking up solidly out of the ground. The roots on the near side barely broke the ground's surface. The tree itself was large and sturdy. I relayed all this information to Dad, secretly hoping that one, I was right, and two, the lesson would be over.

"So?" Dad asked.

"I don't know, Dad. I obviously don't understand what you see."

"Which way do the storms come?"

"From the west—to the left of the tree."

"Right. And?"

"And what? I still don't understand."

"The roots grow larger and more deeply into the ground on the opposite side as the direction of the storms. The roots brace the tree and keep it standing."

Believing the class to be over, I said, "Oh, now I get it, Dad. Thanks."

"Do you?"

"Sure. I see the roots, and I understand what you are saying."

"I don't think so."

"What do you mean?"

"When the storms of life come, we need to have our roots deeply grounded in the Word of God. We will be able to stand against the trials and tribulations of life only if we are grounded and braced against them." Another lesson from nature presented by Dad.

When I think of those lessons, I am reminded of the verse in Jeremiah 1:11–12 (ESV): "The word of the LORD came to me saying, 'What do you see, Jeremiah?' And I said, 'I see a rod of an almond tree.' Then the LORD said to me, 'You have seen well, for I am watching over my word to perform it.'"

Dad was fascinated with trees. Another lesson having to do with their significance was the ice and windstorms that frequented southern Ohio in winter. Once when such a storm had occurred, Dad pointed out that after the ferocious ice storm had covered the trees in heavy encasements of ice, a windstorm followed a day or two later. The wind blew viciously; limbs snapped and crashed to the ground. The woods sounded like a war zone.

Then Dad asked the proverbial question, "Why?"

Again I was powerless to answer his question.

He explained, "The wind and ice are God's way of pruning the trees, taking out the dead branches and limbs that needed to be cut so that the trees take on their new shape."

So I ask you, have you ever seen a beautifully shaped tree in the middle of a field or at the edge of a wood? How did it become so beautifully shaped? God did it! The storms are His pruners.

Could it be that the storms of life are our pruners? We have built up carnal attitudes in our spiritual systems—little sins—and have been AWOL in our relationship with God. We may live this way for days, weeks, even months. God will not keep the relationship in that condition for long, because He yearns to fellowship with us. Thus, the storms begin to brew, and in a short while, trials and tribulations make their appearances. According to John 15:2 (ESV), "Every branch in me that does not bear fruit, he takes away, and every branch that does bear fruit he prunes, that it may bear more fruit." He cuts away the fruitless things and the dead-in-sin branches and restores our fruit-bearing system. I can only believe that Dad would wholeheartedly agree with the lesson I learned in his shadow.

Dad did not share his life lessons just with me. As I mentioned, he was a hunter—a coon hunter most often. He and his hunting buddies—equipped with a good group of dogs and often Mom's pineapple fritters or potato doughnuts and coffee that she would make just for his hunt—would sit on the tailgate of Dad's truck and talk life. Dad would share the Word and his lessons on life from that tailgate. He was instrumental in nine of his hunting buddies becoming Christians, all from the tailgate of a truck while coon hunting. One of the hunters became a preacher of the gospel. Would his buddies have ever known the Lord without Dad's guidance? I wonder.

Later in life, Dad worked as a maintenance custodian in an elementary school. To take such a job after thirty-three years of running his own business was quite an adjustment to his pride. But God had him at the right place at the right time.

In addition to God's providing the right insurance plan to take care of my mother's expensive medical bills, Dad became a teacher of the Word to most of the faculty and staff at the school, especially the principal.

Dad cleared out the furnace room of the basement of the school to be a hangout for him and his supplies. He brought in an old couch, some chairs, and a table for his lunch counter. Soon the teachers and principal invaded his space. There, Dad gave instruction on prayer, finding God's will, and handling problem children, along with countless other lessons of life.

After Dad died, Mom and I received such special messages from these friends. Many of them credited Dad with keeping their marriages and their lives afloat. The principal revered Dad and Mom so much that he named his sons Eli—after Uncle Eli—and Boone—Dad's nickname for my mom.

Dad never was able to be a teacher in a classroom—he would have been great—but God gave him the privilege of teaching countless individuals the true meaning of life and how to live it to God's glory.

I inherited Dad's love of lesson presentation. At this writing, I am nearing fifty years of working in education. Thanks, Dad, for your inheritance of teaching and writing, so that I would have your words and guidance to this very day. Thanks for always being that tall shadow that I played in as a child and stood in through my adult years. Your steps were large and your shadow long. I aspire to continue to walk in them.

PART II

Christlikeness: The Inheritance That Is Ours to Give

CHAPTER 20

Behold, He Stands at the Door and Knocks

NOT A DAY GOES BY THAT I DO NOT IN SOME WAY RECOGNIZE THAT I am standing in the shadows of my inheritance. All I am, or ever will be, I owe to God, the Father; my Lord and Savior, Jesus Christ; the ministering, indwelling Holy Spirit; and my family.

The Scriptures call upon me daily to honor both God and my family with my thoughts, my speech, and my actions. I am, like my family members were, not perfect. I am, like they were, flawed, doing the best I can to live out the Word of God in my daily walk.

Do I always succeed? No.

Am I still a sinner saved by grace? Yes.

Am I always striving to live for Him? Yes, until God calls me home.

Do I live that way exclusively? No. I live that way because the people who cast the shadows in which I walk chose to live that way. Because of their lives modeled before me or narrated to me, I have that rich, godly heritage, and that heritage continues to mold and shape me.

But I have a greater heritage—an adoption into the family of God. My eternal inheritance began on the farm when I was not quite four.

Since I am an only child, I had to entertain myself every day when Mom and Dad were busy. My chief entertainments were playing with my trucks in the coal pile, sitting under the porch and playing in the dirt, and teaching lessons to my captive audience of dolls and stuffed animals.

I would line them up around the foot of my bed, turn my rocking chair on its top to make a lectern-pulpit—teaching or preaching was all the same to me—and teach them their ABCs, numbers, or Bible lessons. I taught my pupils the letters or numbers Mom had taught me or Bible stories from the picture card I had received from Ms. Rose in Sunday school.

One morning, at age three and a half, I preached to my dolls from the latest card. In those days, Sunday school lessons would have a postcard-type lesson with a painting on the front, a verse of Scripture underneath, and the corresponding Bible story on the back. The lesson that week had been Revelation 3:20 (ESV): "Behold, I stand at the door and knock. If anyone hears my voice and opens the door, I will come in to him and eat with him, and he with me."

Ms. Rose, and then my mom, had taught the lesson to me, since I was not old enough to read. I remember liking the lesson, especially because that same picture hung on the wall in my bedroom: Jesus standing at a door with his hand raised to knock. I told my dolls about Jesus's wanting to enter their hearts, in the same way Ms. Rose had explained it to me.

Suddenly, a still small voice—not audible—said to me, *Jeanie, have you ever asked me to come into your heart?*

I remember looking up at the picture on the wall and realizing that Jesus wanted to save me. I did not kneel on the floor or make the usual migration to an altar. I stood staring at the picture on the wall, and I asked Jesus to come into my heart and be my Savior.

It's important to note that I was alone in my bedroom upstairs, so no one was there to tell me what had happened. I recollect that I felt light and free; I was immediately joyful and happy!

I also wanted someone to know about it. I told my dolls first, of course, and then I went running downstairs to tell Mom. She sat down with me on the stairsteps, had me give her the full account, and then explained everything to me. She never suggested that I was too young to understand or tried to dissuade me from believing in the work of Christ in my life that day.

Amazingly, I have the same memory of that eventful day now as I did on the day when I was not quite four years old. On that day, I received my spiritual inheritance.

I had come with childlike faith to God, and I still come in childlike faith today.

Some things in this sin-cursed world require childlike faith. God sees that same need, for He says in Matthew 19:14 (ESV), "But Jesus said, 'Let the little children come to me and do not hinder them, for to such [humility] belongs the kingdom of heaven.'"

He further says in Luke 18:17 (ESV), "Truly, I say to you, whoever does not receive the kingdom of God like a child shall not enter it."

Maybe in our modern, more intellectual times, we make too much of theological understanding. Perhaps childlike faith and acceptance are the very things we need.

For me, as a child I was secure in the knowledge that I was and am a saved individual—that I was and am bound for an eternal heaven with my God. However, Satan would seek to derail my faith and cause me to question my inheritance.

A few years after the picture card incident, the assistant pastor at our Baptist church spoke about the age of accountability. He preached that children from birth to around the age of twelve could not possibly understand what it truly means to be born again. He said that only at the age of accountability could a person understand all that salvation entails and, thus, truly be a child of God. (I question whether we can ever understand all that salvation entails this side of heaven.)

The pastor also said that children under the age of twelve who died would be with God automatically because, at their young age, they had not come to an accountable knowledge of God.

The next Sunday, our senior pastor further commented upon those positions and more precisely explained accountability—especially from the Jewish law perspective—but the damage had already been done to me. Satan began to use my being saved at an immature age as a weapon against me. He planted the doubts that I really did not know what I had done, even though I had a clear memory of that day and my mom had fully explained what it meant to be a Christian. I began doubting that I had ever been saved.

I struggled with that doubt all through my teenage years—years that are hard enough to maintain one's walk with Christ without having salvation doubts. I asked Christ to be my Savior every time an evangelist would come to church for a series of meetings. Out of embarrassment, I never shared with anyone that I kept asking Jesus to be my Savior because everyone believed me to be a Christian. However, each time I tried to be saved again, I never felt the same lightness and joy that I had experienced that first day in my upstairs bedroom.

Finally, when I was twenty-two, an evangelistic team visited our church, and the evangelist asked me to be a counselor for teens at those meetings. I count it a privilege that I counseled one of my own students one night after the service and guided her to an acceptance of the Lord Jesus Christ as her personal Savior.

After she left, I felt crushed by my own doubt and began to cry and pray. My pastor's wife, Mrs. Wahl, was in the same room and had been counseling another teen. She moved over to where I was sitting and took my hand. I stopped praying and opened my eyes to find eyes of compassion staring at me. She asked what was troubling me. I shared that I had been having doubts about my salvation ever since that Sunday when the former assistant pastor had said I could not be saved.

Mrs. Wahl shared that she had been in a similar situation early in her life, having also been saved at a young age. She explained that she was sure I had been saved but that we could nail down the fact that night. We prayed together, and I acknowledged that I had doubted the finished work of Christ, not on the cross but in me.

I affirmed my salvation shortly before my twenty-third birthday, twenty years after the fact, but still I believe with all my heart I had been saved when that still small voice said, *Behold, I stand at the door and knock*.

The shadow of doubt that had ruled my life for many years was gone. I clearly understood I had a godly inheritance from the Lord Jesus Christ, that nothing, not even I, could destroy.

CHAPTER 21

To Some He Gave the Gift of Teaching

I HAVE SPENT FIFTY YEARS OF MY LIFE TEACHING. I CANNOT DO anything else, for God called me to that profession.

As part of our earthly inheritance, God not only establishes our family heritage but also bequeaths to us instruments of service to Him. He means for us to be employed in various occupations according to innate talents, gifts, or personality traits that uniquely equip us for that career. I name that occupation a calling, and it comes from God.

My best illustration of such a calling is the compassionate nurse. A person can readily tell if a nurse has the gift or not, most obviously when they have to perform a task such as drawing blood for tests. I have been privileged to have many called nurses in my life, and I am thankful for them.

Although not a master by any means, because I am still learning, I know God prepared me at a young age to be a teacher. I regularly taught my captive audience of dolls and stuffed animals. I relished the ability to read because, first and most importantly, I could read my Bible stories. I also loved reading because it took me to places outside of Gallia County, like the Far West, England, fairytale lands, and other fantastic places. I would meet new friends in books, so I read all the time.

I shared what I had read with Mrs. Velvie Trotter, my first-grade teacher at Little Bullskin Elementary School. As the old cliché says, in my eyes the sun rose and set on Mrs. Trotter. She loved us all, but she had a special place for me because I was going to be a teacher just like her one day!

Since I went to a three-room elementary school, Mrs. Trotter was also my second-grade teacher. What a privilege! When I left Mrs. Trotter in second grade to advance to third, she gave me my first grown-up book: *Jane Addams.* She inscribed a special message to me inside the front cover, which I especially cherish: "I know you will love your students, and you will make a great teacher."

I wanted more than anything to make Mrs. Trotter proud.

When I finished my first year of teaching, I wrote a letter to Mrs. Trotter telling her of my promised career choice. One day I received a letter in the mail written in a familiar hand. I opened it to find a letter from Mrs. Trotter, who was then in her nineties. She expressed her great joy that I had become a teacher. She closed with, "I know you love your students, and you will be a great teacher."

Mrs. Trotter is with the Lord now, but I still have the treasured letter, and sometimes when I feel down, I pull it out and read it.

At an early age, I quickly became a type A student—the one who conscientiously does her work and worries that it will not be good enough. I longed for the coveted *A.* Dad had instilled that wet-shirt mentality in me; however, it came in the form of, "What did you learn at school today?" And I had better have an answer, or he sent me from the dinner table to find something I could learn quickly. He also taught me that when I placed my head on my pillow at night, I needed to be able to say to the Lord that I had done my best for Him that day.

Some may say that his admonishments were too much for a child to bear, but I think they were needful. I wasn't always able to declare I had done my best, but I faithfully tried to do my best in all that I did and continue to do. His admonitions come directly from Scripture with the shadow of Dad behind it: "And whatsoever ye do, do it heartily as to the Lord, and not unto men. Knowing that of the Lord ye receive the reward of the inheritance, for ye serve the Lord Christ" (Colossians 3:23–24).

I remember working ardently in third grade on a map of the eastern United States. I had drawn symbols of the crops of states and had added a few touches to my map to make it have zing. I drew a whale in the water off the coast of North Carolina. I did not know that whales do not frequent that area of the ocean, but I found them fascinating, so I drew one spouting water.

I cried the night before I was to turn it in, because I was sure Mrs. Brucker would not think it was good enough. She not only thought it good enough to receive an *A+*, but she also displayed it on the wall with the work from fourth and fifth grade. (Remember, I went to a three-room rural school.)

Mom gave me an extra piece of angel food cake at dinner for doing such an excellent job. As he was inclined to do, Dad did not praise me but just reminded me that if I had done my best, that was the important thing. I never could quite escape that shadow of excellence Dad expected.

Although I dabbled with other possibilities for a career choice—nurse, artist, bank teller, and even pilot—I never strayed far from the desire to be a teacher. I completed my secondary education language arts degree at Rio Grande College, now the University of Rio Grande, and began teaching at my alma mater. My experience there was miserable. Looking back now, I see that I was far from being a teacher. I occupied a classroom, created artistic bulletin boards, and fraternized with students. I thought I was teaching, but I doubt my students from those years can truthfully say they learned English and speech from me.

I ashamedly apologize to all my students from those three years. I had been taught progressive teaching—to be a pal to students—and I readily complied. I have since learned and experienced that students need a teacher, not a friend. A teacher can only become a student's friend *after* being a teacher to them.

Many of my former students are friends of mine today. I believe that the shadow of a faithful mother and best friend prepared me for that lesson.

By His grace, God had a plan to teach me what it means to be a teacher. I learned how to teach while pursuing my master's degree in educational administration at Bob Jones University. I also learned about Christian education there. I knew little of the Christian school movement until I went to Bob Jones. My education had come the standard way: secular education with strong biblical teaching from my family.

After teaching at Bob Jones, I moved to be closer to my family, as my mom was having serious health issues at the time. I began teaching at Cross Lanes Christian School as an ideological English and speech teacher. Since I had learned so much about education, and particularly effective teaching, I was confidently prepared to instruct my students on becoming "perfect" Christians. I subsequently set higher expectations for the Christian school students than I had previously expected from public-school students.

The result was flagrant disappointment. These students were sometimes liars, cheaters, disrespectful minions, and cruel jokesters—not at all what one would expect in a Christian school. They were those things because they were flawed human beings with sin natures, just like their teacher, and they succumbed to the old nature from time to time.

As a newly graduated master teacher, I sought to reform them—to press them into the preconceived mold I had for saintly Christian students.

On the weekends I spent with Mom and Dad, I would relate the latest horror story and tell them how I had championed the cause of Christ in reforming my students. I also shared that some of my plans were not coming to fruition.

Dad, in his slow, bass voice, said something like, "Did you sign a contract with Cross Lanes Christian?"

"Yes, of course," I replied.

"What does that contract say you are hired to do?"

"Teach English and speech."

"Then quit trying to reform those kids. Teach what you were hired to teach, and model Christ before them in your teaching."

That was one of the many nuggets of wisdom my dad passed on to me as I continued my teaching career. From that day on, I sought to teach English and speech with all my might and to model Christ with all His strength. I recognized through Dad's admonishment that I had been pridefully trying to do everything in my own strength, which was failing miserably.

I had also set myself up as judge and jury over my students using a set of standards only God could fulfill. I lacked grace and mercy for both my students and me. Second Corinthians 12:9 says, "My grace is sufficient for thee: for my strength is made perfect in weakness. Most gladly therefore will I rather glory in my infirmities, that the power of Christ may rest upon me."

I was not in any way accounting for God's design of each individual student. I had determined what they should talk like, walk like, and even smell like. I came to realize that I needed His grace to model His Word and His guidance to meet my students' intellectual, emotional, and spiritual needs.

The burden of trying to be all things to my students lifted that day. Although it took longer for the second phase—the preconceived set of standards for judgment—to ease, I soon relaxed with my students and began to enjoy teaching and being with them. I viewed them and myself as God's handiwork. We all were works in progress.

The shadow of that godly inheritance Dad had bequeathed—the wet-shirt mentality—became the foundation for the beginning of each new year, the guide for each life challenge the students and I faced together, and the go-to thought for fine arts competitions, stage productions, and academic challenges. I embraced Colossians 3:23: "And whatsoever ye do, do it *heartily*!" (emphasis added by author).

The first attempt I made to instill that principle in my students one year was in the customary introduction of myself at the beginning of class. I took this time to share my salvation story.

Without referencing my dad's instruction on doing one's best, I then guided my students in a dramatic recitation of Colossians 3:23–24. I began by having the students recite the verses with me. When they arrived at the word *heartily,* their tone was rather lackluster. I stopped them and dramatically suggested that they put more *umph* in their speech.

We started over and arrived at the word again. They did a little better, but they still had not attained the level I was searching for.

Finally, after three or four tries, they successfully yelled, "Heartily!!!" That hearty yell summoned the principal from the hall, no doubt to quiet our rambunctious clamor. Red-faced, I explained the noise, and he smiled and sat down to listen. I felt my teaching career might be in danger of ceasing at that moment. Rationality told me to move on to the guidelines for classroom behavior, but I had a more urgent message for the students. We once again began recounting the verses, but this time with a quieter approach.

I stopped the students at junctures in the verses, especially at "as to the Lord, and not unto men" and "for ye serve the Lord Christ," explaining the urgency of doing all things for the Lord and not for the praise of men.

In later years and at a different school, this concept became a regular prayer for me and my students before each major school event: "Lord, we are performing our best today for an audience of one; if you are pleased, we will be pleased."

I received an inheritance from my dad in whose shadow I attempt to walk: seek to please the Lord with your labor every day. I so wanted to pass that inheritance on to my students.

A few years ago, at a fine arts competition, I discovered a circle of my students praying for their upcoming performance. One of my gifted young men was leading the group.

He concluded his prayer with, "Today, Lord, we are performing for an audience of one. We pray you will be pleased. Help us, Lord, to deliver the message the best that we can. The results are in your hands."

I caught a glimpse of a shadow that day. It was my own. What an inheritance to pass to my students!

CHAPTER 22

Send Them Forth

AMONG OTHER EXTRACURRICULAR DUTIES AT CROSS LANES, I coached cheerleading. I had never been a cheerleader or aspired to be one for that matter. However, in Christian education, leaders often ask teachers and staff members to step out of their comfort zones. Cheerleading coach was a title not remotely in my comfort zone!

Cheerleaders not only traveled with the ball teams, but they also had their own competitions. We would travel to tournaments on a school van, hauling a cargo trailer behind that held all our luggage and gear. We never traveled anywhere without asking the Lord to protect us and to help us reflect Him in our travels.

I would tell the girls before we left, "Remember whose you are."

People often develop extensively used catch phrases, never imagining that they are making any kind of impact upon the listeners. Such was this phrase for me. I just wanted my girls to understand what my father had taught me. I was a Stewart, and I was never to bring a reproach upon that name or the name of the Lord Jesus by living other than as a representative of my family's and His name: Stewart and Christian. I am sure I have disappointed in both, but it was never my intention.

Years after my cheerleading experience, I connected with one of my Cross Lanes students, a woman named Heather, through Facebook. She reminded me of the encouragement I had always given the girls.

Then she said, "Miss Stewart, I never allow my own children to leave home without reminding them whose they are."

I am so abundantly proud of her and her children, for she and her husband have established shadows for their children to walk in, and they are doing just that. Heather and Bill are building a godly inheritance to leave to their children and their children's children. Praise the Lord!

Traveling with a group of teenage girls can be a great deal of fun, but such travel can also be a source of jealousies, pettiness, and outright conflict. I don't recall the occasion or which year that I tried my hand at drafting a cheer, but nevertheless, I did. The cheer came as a result of some harsh words exchanged between two of my senior girls. They were head cheerleaders, and both had strong opinions. Satan was having a party at my squad's expense.

I gathered the team together in my room and asked them to sit down. Then I addressed the issue, pointing out that they were not only representatives of the school but also of Christ. I added that they were also being watched by the squads of other schools and, no doubt, the tournament judges.

"Displays of anger and complaint are an open opportunity for Satan to attack and destroy our reputation," I exhorted.

Then I made up a cheer on the spot and presented it to the girls, without stunts or gestures, I might add. The cheer was as follows:

Go, Satan! Flee!
You cannot win!
Christ has won the vic-to-ry!
Go, Satan! Flee!

The girls gazed at me in astonishment until one of the seniors burst into guffaws of laughter. "Oh, Ms. Stewart! Don't give up your day job!"

The tension in the room lessened. Regardless of the roars of laughter, the girls comprehended the message. We give Satan too much room in our lives for his attack. He uses any means to distract us from our goal: to follow after Christ.

Several years later, I was addressing a group of women at a ladies' retreat. One of the ladies asked a question about how to successfully battle Satan and win. I took the ladies to James 4:7: "Resist the devil, and he will flee from you." I then told the story of how I had made up a cheer for those cheerleaders years before.

The same young lady then asked, "Would you share it?"

With a knowing smile, I replied, "I am not sure you are ready for it."

The group simultaneously begged, "Please!"

Laying aside my better judgment, I began. "Go, Satan! Flee! You cannot win! Christ has won the vic-to-ry! Go, Satan! Flee!"

Smiles and restrained fits of laughter followed.

Then the young lady asked, "Could you say that again? I want to write it down."

It may seem silly to us to resort to such tactics, but I believe we give too much ground to the devil. For the Christian, sin comes by invitation only, meaning we accept the temptation in rebellion to God and willingly commit the sin. We could have just as easily said, "Satan, leave and take your temptation with you!"

If God's Word is true, and it is, then he has no choice but to flee when we tell him to go.

Being a cheerleading coach, unwittingly as it was, gave me many opportunities to cast a shadow for my girls. Each time I sent them forth, they knew they belonged to God and that He was victorious over sin so that they could walk in the Spirit and not after the flesh. They knew Satan had to obey when they said, "Go!"

As a teacher, I have a tremendous responsibility to teach from biblical principle, whether in public or Christian school classrooms. I have spent equal time teaching in both areas. Whether I teach Sunday school or a group of teachers, God has exhorted me to present the truth of Scripture and to view this world from a biblical standpoint.

It says in Ephesians 4:11–16 (ESV):

And he gave the apostles, the prophets, the evangelists, the shep-
herds and teachers, to equip the saints for the work of ministry,
for building up the body of Christ, until we all attain to the
unity of the faith and of the knowledge of the Son of God,
to mature manhood [or womanhood], to the measure of the

stature of the fullness of Christ, so that we may no longer be children, tossed to and fro by the waves and carried about by every wind of doctrine, by human cunning, by craftiness in deceitful schemes [Satan's attacks]. Rather, speaking the truth in love, we are to grow up in every way into him who is the head, into Christ, from whom the whole body, joined and held together by every joint with which it is equipped, when each part is working properly, makes the body grow so that it builds itself up in love.

I have not married, nor have I had children of my own. Frankly, at times I have questioned the Lord about what was wrong with me that I remained an "unclaimed blessing." Oftentimes, the troubling questions came after someone asked me why I had never married.

One day, a devotional by Charles Spurgeon led me to Isaiah 54. These verses came after one of those self-reflecting, self-deprecating times. "Sing, O barren one, who did not bear; break forth into singing and cry aloud, you who have not been in labor! For the children of the desolate one *will be more than the children of her who is married*, says the Lord" (Isaiah 54:1 ESV, emphasis added by author).

Emotions suddenly overwhelmed me. The magnitude of God's provision and the surety of His calling overshadow me. God has blessed me with countless children under my teaching. I have stopped counting the number of students, old and young, who have crossed the threshold into my classroom.

God gave the power, the Lord Jesus Christ gave me the instruction, and the Holy Spirit gave me the gift. I thank Him every day for the privilege to step into a classroom.

My earnest prayer is that all my students realized my love for them as I sent them forth. I pray I have been salt and light to them. I trust and pray that they walk in the shadow of His light, and as they send out their children, they will establish a godly inheritance for their children so that their children's children will recognize their shadows and will walk in them.

CHAPTER 23

An Inheritance Undefiled That Fadeth Not Away

IF YOU RECALL, I TOOK A SHADOW AS A PLAYTHING WHEN I WAS quite young. Then a "monster" overtook my playmate. That monster was my dad, whose stature loomed greater than my own.

One might define a shadow as an image created by a light source positioned at just the right angle to produce a shaded silhouette of the person or thing. Shadows must have a light source. Jesus Christ has been the light source for the shadows that my grandparents and parents cast.

Although I have received all those marvelous gifts bequeathed to me from these God-fearing folks, I have received a far more marvelous inheritance: "An inheritance that is imperishable, undefiled, and unfading, kept in heaven for [me]" (1 Peter 1:4 ESV). Because my grandparents, father, and mother all knew the Father through the Son, the Lord Jesus Christ, by the power of the Holy Spirit, they had this enduring inheritance, reserved and secured in heaven for them. Because I accepted the Lord Jesus Christ as my Savior, I, too, have that inheritance reserved and secured in heaven for me. One day I will see my loved ones, and greater than that blessing is the fact that I will see my Savior face to face.

Let me make one point clear here—I have that inheritance not because of anything I have done, nor through the prayers of my parents (although my family regularly uttered prayers for me), nor through a church denomination. I have a secure salvation through faith in the finished work of Jesus Christ—His death, His burial, and His resurrection. He is "the [only] way, the truth, and the life; no man [or woman or child] cometh unto the Father, but by me (John 14:6).

After shadow-casting, the second aspect of this metaphorical discussion is *inheritance*.

If we are to cast a shadow of Christlikeness, we must understand the role of inheritance biblically and know that as benefactors, we must seek to win others to Christ as our legacy to this world. As Christ was the Light of salvation, so we are identified as light to the world (Matthew 5:14).

I remember distinctly the day that the term *inheritance* intrigued me to the point that I began a biblical study of the word.

My friend Abby Shields was speaking at a ladies' retreat at our church. During the course of her presentations, she gave each of us a neon pink card that read, "Who I Am in Christ." I tucked it away in my Bible and continued assisting with the program.

A few days later, I pulled the placard out during my devotions and read through the blessings of knowing Christ as my Savior. Since I had always had a love-hurt relationship with my dad, I was particularly struck by the words, "Accepted in the beloved" (Ephesians 1:6). I remember crying with joy over those words. God accepted me and loved me because of Christ; these words were His love letter to me!

If that realization wasn't enough, a few lines later was the message, "Joint-heir with Jesus Christ." Now, I knew the verses that we have "an inheritance incorruptible, and undefiled, and that fadeth not away, reserved in heaven for [me]" (1 Peter 1:4), and "If children, then heirs; heirs of God, and joint-heirs with Christ; if so be that we suffer with him, that we may be also glorified together" (Romans 8:17). I knew them literally—true— but I had never really taken stock of what the verses meant in application.

Those verses prompted questions: As a joint heir of Jesus Christ, do I receive the same from the Father that Christ receives? How is that inheritance incorruptible and undefiled? What do these truths mean? I, consequently, began a study on inheritance and what it meant for me. I am supremely glad I did! Here is some of what I learned.

When my parents died, their wills named me as their beneficiary, and I received an inheritance. I had no part in accumulating that inheritance; they merely named me as a recipient of it. All I had to do to receive it was to hear the will read and to sign the necessary documents.

Our spiritual inheritance parallels this life experience. With our heavenly inheritance, we Christians also have no part in establishing our inheritance bequeathed through salvation. We receive the inheritance as we hear the Word—comparable to a will—and place our trust in God, accepting His Son as redemptive Savior and Lord of our lives. God then scribes our names in the Book of Life—an affirmation of that will—as confirmed in Revelation 13:8: "And all that dwell upon the earth shall worship him [the beast], whose names are *not* written in the book of life of the Lamb slain from the foundation of the world" (emphasis added by author).

Through the inheritance study, I became even more convinced that no salvation experience is grand enough to warrant that salvation. It is not the experience that saves. While we must exercise faith to believe all that salvation involves, it is Christ's salvation to give—not ours to achieve. Neither is the degree of our faith a requirement for this salvation, for our measurement of faith is not in keeping with God's measure, which as Christ taught His disciples is childlike in its humility. We come to Him as humble, lost sinners in need of His saving power. We then cannot boast of our salvation experience, for salvation is all the work of Christ.

Let us further reason together. If our salvation were dependent upon our faith, then our salvation would waver as our faith wavers. If our salvation were dependent upon our works for Him, that salvation would waver as much as our service for Him wavers. Even further, if our salvation were dependent upon our works, how would we ever be assured that we had worked enough to warrant being saved?

Since it is impossible for our works to be steadfast or sufficient, we must conclude, as Scripture does: "For by grace you have been saved through faith. And this is not of your own doing; it is the gift of God: not a result of works, so that no one may boast" (Ephesians 2:8–9 ESV).

I remember when I reasoned out these things, I said aloud, "Praise the Lord!"

I have the salvation of the Lord. Through that salvation, I have gained an inheritance. Further study would be necessary to know what that inheritance contains and how it contributes to the Christlikeness we are to model in our Christian walk.

Galatians 4:4–5 (ESV) exposits that inheritance: "But when the fullness of time had come, God sent forth His Son, born of a woman, born under the law, to redeem those who were under the law, so that we might receive the *adoption* as sons [children] of the Father" (emphasis added by author).

Regardless of the family I had on earth—praise God, I had a wonderful one—I am a part of a grander and more immense family of God. Thus, when I accepted the Lord as Savior, I became God's child, adopted into His family: "But as many as received him, to them gave he power to become the sons [daughters] of God, even to them that believe on his name" (John 1:12).

As a child of God, I have then the inheritance that goes to any family member. I am a joint heir with Jesus Christ, according to Romans 8:14–17 ESV:

> For all who are led by the Spirit of God are sons [and daughters] of God. For you did not receive the spirit of slavery to fall back into fear, but you have received the Spirit of adoption as sons, by whom we cry, "Abba! Father!" The Spirit himself bears witness with our spirit that we are children of God, and if children, then heirs—heirs of God and fellow heirs with Christ, provided we suffer with him in order that we may also be glorified with him.

As I have received an earthly inheritance through my parents' will, I have received a spiritual inheritance through the adoption process made possible through the finished work of Jesus Christ. It is God's will that His created ones be adopted into His family. Thus, I belong to two families— the earthly family that cast such wonderful shadows, and a heavenly family that was the source of light for those shadows. Praise the triune God!

Biblically, I can draw a parallel of both inheritance and adoption to a legal process—the adoption and inheritance together as the will of God interpreted by the law.

I am, by law, an only child; however, by family line, I am the oldest of two children. As I related earlier, I had a sister who was stillborn, who would have been eight years my junior. The loss of Judith Gail devastated my parents and me. The span of eight years between my birth and hers indicated the difficulty my parents had in conceiving. By God's will, they did not have another child of their own.

They did, however, contemplate adopting a boy—a child of a family we knew. The loss of the mother to cancer left her six children for the father to raise. He felt incapable of handling such an awesome responsibility and chose to put the children up for adoption. Three families considered adopting the children. As friends, we all wanted the children to be able to see each other as regularly as possible.

Since our financial circumstances would not allow us to adopt more than one of the children, we sought to adopt one of the boys who we were particularly close to. The other families chose three and two of the children, respectively.

Dad and Mom started the proceedings under law but soon learned that the state would not release the boy for adoption, due to a preexisting physical condition that required he remain in the care of the state of Ohio. I don't recall all of the technical determinants of the law, but he had a weak heart with a murmur, among other difficulties.

The two families did adopt the other five children, and thankfully, they made sure that the boy we had wanted had regular visits with his siblings. Had we been able to adopt this boy, he would have been a part of our family—a son and brother—and would have had an equal inheritance with me. His adoption would have secured his place in the Stewart family by love and by law.

Having gone through that experience, I could readily connect the legal adoption process with the biblical definition. In the same way we began this process of adoption, sinners go through an adoption process when they accept the Lord Jesus Christ as their own personal Savior.

This adoption into God's family is much like an earthly adoption, as Paul describes in his letters to the various churches. Paul presents adoption in legal terms, some of which we will look at together.

I am a teacher, not a lawyer, but I have had some limited experience in the law world. I have sold property on my own, set up a will on my own, and worked one summer in a law office.

My job at the law firm was to attempt, in a brief amount of time, to school lawyers on communicating with their constituents in layman's terms. Most of their outgoing letters read like a legal brief and required a lawyer, or at least a law clerk, to decipher the message. The lawyers were so in tune with their jargon that they were oblivious that their clients were unable to understand *lawyerese.*

Granted, by law, some of the vocabulary within the letters could not change, but the communication between lawyer and client had to be clearly understood. In one incident, one of the firm's major clients had a concern, causing the owner to recognize the need to communicate more effectively. Realizing that ineffective communication put the livelihood or economic future of clients at stake, the law firm created my position to fill this need.

Much like this office experience in communication, Paul presents the believer's position in Christ from a law perspective, converting *lawyerese* to layman's terms. As an adopted child of God, I receive all the benefits in the family of God as the Son, the firstborn of many sons (redeemed ones).

Some people believe in circumstances just being that—circumstances. I believe God often orchestrates circumstances for our instruction. I had taught AP Language and Composition and AP Literature and Composition for over twenty years. Oftentimes, I must confess I learned more than my students. The teacher must plow through quite advanced reading and must spend time deeply studying the text and its implications. Of course, the selections are ninety-nine percent secular works, but to God all things are sacred. He will use the secular to highlight His sacred message.

One day I was preparing a practice exam for my students; the reading for a set of questions concerned the Roman familial relationship. In the past, I had read these passages and answered the questions to anticipate any difficulties my students might have. This time as I was reading, the connection between Roman law's definition of family and the biblical definition of family struck me. The passage related that the position of adopted son in Roman law (reflecting Paul's audience in the New Testament, by the way) was uniquely different from Old Testament law. The adopted son in Roman law was the chief inheritor of the estate and had the right to the name and citizenship of the person who adopted him. (The law, incidentally, did not provide for daughters, only sons.) In addition, the law bestowed upon the adoptive parents the full care of the child: *authority* over the child, *responsibility* for the child, and *entitlement* to the child.

Excited about this new "circumstantial" revelation, I reread the passage, solely with a biblical view in mind. While reading this second time, I began to draw a biblical parallel. God's sovereignty has admittedly been an enigma for me as it relates to man's free will. Oftentimes, the two would seem in conflict. Thus, I asked, "What does that law descriptor 'all authority (sovereign control) over our lives' mean?"

He gave me this answer through further study. I began with excitement to see that God's authority has full responsibility to provide all necessities and obligations for the adopted one. That's me! Regardless of my earthly parentage, God wants to be my loving heavenly Father and be the provider of all my needs. For that parentage to occur, He sent His one and only Son to be the means of adoption, and then He provides everything I need for this earthly life and the life to come after death. He becomes the authority over my life, much like the legal authority my parents had over me, only greater.

Our earthy parents—despite their attempts—are or were flawed human beings, sinners in need of a Savior. Perhaps they may not have been godly examples or trusted ones as mine were; however, God is perfect, flawless, and full of all authority in heaven and earth. He is worthy as our Creator and as the perfect righteous Father to be trusted in all matters of life. By His love, He loads us with benefits as Father to children.

In love, God also does not force us to become His children. We are not puppets in the hands of a puppeteer. He leaves the choice to our will. It is our decision to accept or not to accept His authority.

In a movie I watched some time ago—the title eludes—the chief character had lost his first wife to cancer and was raising his son on his own. He had met a widow who also had children by her first marriage. Wisely, the soon-to-be husband asked the soon-to-be bride's children if they would allow him to marry their mother. He had also previously asked his son if he would accept his new bride. He sought their desires in the marriage. Thankfully for him they said, "Yes!" unanimously. The wise groom did not force his will upon the children but allowed them to make the choice.

I realize the movie was a fictional scenario, but with God the choice is not fictional. It is the reality of His sovereignty and our will.

We are God's twice if we have accepted His redemptive plan through His beloved Son.

He first created us in His image—that is the image of the triune God, of course. He also designed the plan of salvation. And He, through that salvation, adopted us into His family. We became sisters and brothers of the Lord Jesus Christ and, as such, we gained a godly inheritance as a joint heir with Him. Though I am an only child, I am part of a grand family of believers here on earth and in heaven.

This fact reminds me of a story. A father and his son had built a toy boat together. Under the father's guidance, the boy would sail the little boat down the neighborhood stream. Soon the father allowed his son to sail the boat alone.

"Now, son, don't sail your boat when the stream is high. It might get away from you."

The boy nodded in reply.

Later, after a summer rain, the temptation to sail his boat became too much for the boy. He launched the boat in the risen water. Soon the boat escaped his reach and eventually also his sight as he ran along the stream.

That night the boy had to tell his father of the mishap.

"I'm sorry, son. I warned you about not sailing your boat in high water. I am afraid it is lost."

A few weeks later, the boy and his mother were shopping in town, and the boy saw his toy boat displayed in a store window. The boy and his mother entered the store.

"Mister, that boat is mine!" the boy exclaimed, as he pointed to the window.

"No, son, I'm sorry, but I bought that boat, so I am afraid it belongs to me. If you want it, you will need to buy it."

"How much is it?" the boy asked.

The man told him the price. The boy did not have the money, but he went home and worked at odd jobs for his parents and neighbors to raise the necessary money. Finally, he had the amount needed.

He returned to the store and laid down the money for the treasured boat.

He hugged the boat to his chest and exclaimed as he left the store, "Mine twice!"

We who know the Lord as Savior are His twice, through creation and through redemption.

No one in the body of believers in Christ doubts the magnitude of salvation. In fact, we so recognize its importance that we seek to tell others the good news of the gospel. Just as I, as a near four-year-old child, delighted to tell others of Christ, I am to delight in doing so today. We who know the Lord have a responsibility to leave a legacy of that inheritance "undefiled that fadeth not away, reserved in heaven" for us and those of the next generation.

CHAPTER 24

Paid in Full

I AM A LIST MAKER! I ALWAYS GO TO THE GROCERY STORE WITH A shopping list and a pencil if I am in my right mind. If I don't have said list, I do one of two things, or maybe both: I forget an important item or items, or I buy what I didn't intend to buy, most often things that are not good for me. I live by the list.

When I clean house, I list my chores by room and delight in checking off each item as completed. I learned early on to carry things from another room into their proper room and place as I move through my chores. Displaced articles clutter a room.

When I prepare lessons, I make a list of the objectives, the procedure, and the ancillaries I will need for the lesson. I check off each item as I complete the preparation. If I have successfully adhered to my list, the lesson will run smoothly. I discovered in teaching, if I don't have a plan, my students will.

Unfortunately, however, list making had a negative impact on my early spiritual adulthood. But through that displaced way of thinking that cluttered my view of God's grace, I discovered God's plan rather than mine.

Having grown up in the church of the seventies, I succumbed to the ascribed teaching of the fundamental, Bible-believing church of the day. At best, that teaching bestowed upon me a desire to study my Bible, to claim God's promises found there, and to gather with other people of like faith and practice regularly. I made assurance of my salvation, became active in my local church, and dedicated my life to serving the Lord during this period.

At worst, I fulfilled a list of dos and don'ts guaranteed to maintain my standing in Christ. Now mind you, my father and I had participated in numerous conversations about security of the believer versus works for salvation, and I wholeheartedly held to security of the believer. I still fell victim, however, to the legalistic belief that I somehow had to earn my standing in Christ. I believe the wet-shirt teaching and the American way of working to achieve contributed to a misunderstanding of my role in my spiritual walk.

I came to understand later that the checklist mentality of serving the Lord is termed *legalism*. Legalistic practice meant that as I placed my head on my pillow each night, I would check off all the good things I had done that day and figuratively wipe my brow that I had not committed any serious don'ts.

My conversational prayer might sound like this: Devotions? Check. Prayer? Check. Greeted others with a smile? Check. Prepared my lessons well? Check. Managed my temper in a trying situation? Check. Murdered? No! Stole? No! Cheated? No! Phew! I was good today!

I took confidence that I had done my best without recognizing that I had kept the law. This practice fit right in with my penchant for list-making and living by it! What I garnered from such practice was a false sense of my own importance and, at times, a critical spirit marked by a judgmental attitude.

With legalism, I became self-sufficient, even pharisaical, and proud that I had scored well on my checklist. I was living out my salvation instead of living in the salvation that is only Christ's.

After reading works from authors such as C. S. Lewis, Charles Ryrie, and John Bunyan, I began being instructed by the Holy Spirit on a word seemingly missing from the practice of legalism: *grace*.

Grace is the foundation for Christ's salvation in all who accept the Son of God as Savior. God so loved the world that He, by grace, sought His human creation to be a part of His family. He "commendeth His love toward us, in that, while we were yet sinners, Christ died for us" (Romans

5:8). Interestingly, I never sought Christ. He came seeking me—seeking the treasure for whom He was willing to die.

Treasures are valuable possessions. On my twelfth birthday, my parents gave me a birthstone ring—an aquamarine. It was a beautiful ring, and I treasured it. I treasured it so much that I wore it when I shouldn't have . . . all the time.

One day my neighbor friend, Mitzi, and I tromped through high weeds and remains of a garden, heading to a friend's house for a pickup game of softball. I was halfway across the patch of ground refuse when I looked down and saw that my ring was missing.

"Mitzi! Stop! I have lost my ring!" I frantically yelled. "Help me find it!"

"Oh no! Where do you think you lost it?" she shouted in response.

"Somewhere around here!"

"Are you kidding me? We will never find it in this mess!"

"I can't go with you now. I have to find my ring!"

Mitzi hung around for a while, sweeping through the tall weeds until she finally gave up and left me in my grief.

I ran to the house, then burst in to tell my parents the dreadful news.

"We'll find it," my mother spoke assuredly.

"Don't tell her that!" my truth-telling father exclaimed. "You will never find the ring; it's lost."

"Well, we will go look just to make sure," my mom responded.

Now, my mother had the uncanny ability to find four-leaf clovers by just walking barefoot through a patch and looking down. I could be on my hands and knees scouring the yard, but she would just spy one and pick it right in front of my nose.

Together, we swept the area.

Just as I was affirming my father's prediction, my mom yelled, "I found it!"

Crying, I ran to her and put the treasured ring on my finger.

I stammered out, "I knew you would find it."

I am of greater value to God than my ring was to me. I can almost imagine my heavenly Father saying the same when I accepted His Son as my Savior: "I knew you would find it!" What did I find when I found the

Lord as my Savior? I found a list of treasures that came not through my efforts but through the beneficent grace of Jesus: the benefits of knowing Him. When I discovered grace, I discovered a freeing treasure!

One of the many freeing benefits of being adopted into the family of God through salvation is *justification*, a legal term. So let's view it from a legal perspective.

I worked my way through college as a bank teller in the summers and holidays. After my fellow employees and I closed the branch bank for the day, we would make our way to the home bank in town. There we would turn in the day's transactions and assume a second job to finish our daily hours. I worked in the real estate loan department, posting payments and justifying the day's receipts. At the posting machine, I entered each payment, divided by principal and interest (the interest always being higher than the principal), and affixed the new total due on the account. It was a celebratory day when customers made their last payment and the ledger would be stamped, "Paid in full." They had labored and paid off the debt they owed to the bank. The property was now theirs.

Like most adult Americans, I have accrued indebtedness. I have a mortgage, and one day I will make the final payment on the property and have full ownership of my home. The transaction will also read, "Paid in full."

In like manner, I have a sin debt. Because of the righteousness of God, He has deemed me guilty before the Law: the judgment against me is guilty, and the sentence is eternity in hell. Yet in His great love for me, He provided a way of salvation by which I am set free from that debt. Instead of hell, I will spend eternity in heaven with God. That way is Jesus Christ who, though sinless, purchased my pardon from sin through His death on the cross. The judgment against me and all who place their trust in His finished work—the death, burial, and resurrection—is pronounced. Paid in full forever. That is justification. As the old Sunday school adage reads, "Just as if I had never sinned."

With mortgages, I and others labor to pay off the indebtedness, paying back to the institution interest for carrying the debt for me. With God's plan of salvation, I did not labor, nor am I able to pay back interest on the sin debt I owe. Only through Christ can my debt be paid once for all time. Salvation, then, becomes the treasured gift.

Paul addresses this justification in Romans 3:23–25 (ESV):

> For all have sinned and fall short of the glory of God, and are *justified* by his *grace* as a *gift*, through the redemption that is in Christ Jesus, whom God put forward as a propitiation [reconciliation] by his blood, to be received by faith. This was to show God's righteousness, because in his divine forbearance he had passed over [covered] former sins. (emphasis added by author)

The sinless One became the propitiation for our sinfulness through His shed blood. And yet we become a joint heir with Him—a double portion of benefit.

Justification is that singular moment at salvation when you step out of the dark shadow of condemnation into the light of His grace and receive an inheritance undefiled. God's grace produces this justification benefit of salvation, not by my list of good deeds or the absence of horrible sins. Legalism clutters God's graciousness.

Another benefit associated with salvation is *reconciliation,* a restoring of relationship.

My father had an unusual way of demonstrating reconciliation when he felt a sin had been committed against him, Mom, or anyone else. When I was little and did something wrong, he disciplined me with a talking to or sometimes a spanking.

Then my father became distant. He would sit in his chair, and I would approach his chair, look at him, and he would look back at me but keep his silence.

Next, I would sit down at his feet and look up at him, and he would once again avert his eyes. Slowly, I would crawl up on his lap, yet he still would not acknowledge my presence. Then I would put my arms around his neck and confess that I had done the offensive thing and that I was sorry. Dad would return the hug with an extra pat, and all would be forgiven.

I am not presenting this method as one that parents need to embrace. I am merely showing that the repentant heart was what my dad was looking for. I did not understand that at the time, but I did long for that reconciled relationship with my father. When I sin now, I still want that reconciled relationship, but this time with my heavenly Father.

In teaching I often talk to students about this idea of repentance. In one class I was reviewing a lesson that had illustrated repentance. I asked the students what repentance was, and one student answered that it was turning a three-sixty from sin. Recognizing his gaffe, we all laughed. Of course, 360 degrees would land us right back where we were. Contrastingly, a repentant heart turns from the sin and toward the Savior in a 180-degree turn.

So how does that one-eighty occur?

"If [I] confess [my] sin, he is faithful and just to forgive [me] of [my] sin and to cleanse [me] from all unrighteousness" (1 John 1:9 ESV). God is waiting for me to agree with Him about the sin I have committed. I am to have the same abhorrence for sin that He possesses. Because of His holiness and His view of my sin, He expects godly sorrow for that sin and a desire to turn from it to Him. The Bible calls this action *repentance*. My repentant heart indicates that I am turning 180 degrees from that sin, and in godly sorrow for it, I determine to abandon that sin by God's grace and help. Reconciliation is possible through confessing the sin and through a heart that recognizes the exorbitant cost of forgiveness. But without the gracious intercession of Christ on my behalf, that sin would remain unforgiven and the relationship with the Father distant.

Once again, Paul uses legal terminology to drive home the point: "Who is to condemn? Christ Jesus is the one who died—more than that, who was raised—who is at the right hand of God, who indeed is interceding for us" (Romans 8:34 ESV). Jesus Christ, through His shed blood, is the lawyer who defends us before God. He pleads our case when we sin. Even if we have not confessed, His forgiveness is still freely given, waiting for our understanding and confession—the figurative arms around His neck and a due confession.

I am afraid, however, that today we Christians have often lost the truth of turning a one-eighty and have exchanged it for a three-sixty. We may be sorry that we have been caught in our sin, or we truly may be sorry for the sin, but then we continue to feel an overwhelming desire for that sin. In that case, after confession and agreeing with God that it is a grievous sin, we do a three-sixty and wind up right back where we were—committing the same sin. Godly sorrow is missing, which then causes fellowship with the Father to be strained and even silent.

When someone speaks of broken fellowship, I think of the words of Christ from the cross. Christ, bearing our sin that God could not look upon, cried out, "My God, my God, why hast thou forsaken me?" (Matthew 27:46). For that moment in time, the Father of heaven and His only begotten Son were not in fellowship because of sin.

Living independently in our three-sixty thinking is a skewed interpretation of living a trusting and obedient life in response to God's love for us. So, too, is the viewpoint with its list of dos and don'ts.

Is this the legacy we want to leave to children? A legacy that lives in the three-sixty? A legacy of broken fellowship with the Father of heaven?

As aforementioned, the benefit that most strongly associates with the theme of this book is a familial relationship, which is astoundingly important to me. Thus, please allow me to present four additional benefits Christ has bestowed upon us in His family

First, as an adopted child of God, I now have a heavenly Father, not a righteous judge. No condemnation comes to me now, for Christ has redeemed me and made me a joint heir with Him.

> There is therefore now no condemnation to them which are in Christ Jesus, who walk not after the flesh [keeping the list], but after the Spirit. For the law of the Spirit of life in Christ Jesus hath made me free from the law of sin and death . . . God sending his own Son in the likeness of sinful flesh . . . condemned sin in the flesh: That the righteousness of the law might be fulfilled in us, who walk not after the flesh, but after the Spirit (Romans 8:1–4).

Because of the intercession of the Lord Jesus Christ, I can boldly come to the Father anytime, day or night. My heavenly Father is fully accessible.

As an adopted child, I have a kinship with Jesus Christ, which is the second familiar benefit. Nothing that I go through in this life has not been touched, felt, or experienced by Jesus Himself. He took on flesh so that He might fully know humanity. Hebrews 4:15 says, "For we have not a high priest which cannot be touched with the feeling of our infirmities; but was in all points tempted like as we are, yet without sin."

The old hymn "I Stand Amazed" says it quite well: "He took my sins and my sorrows, He made them His very own; He bore the burden to Calv'ry, He suffered and died alone." Jesus does not just sympathize; in His humanity, He empathizes with His earthly brothers and sisters.

Sympathy for another is quite different from empathy with another. After my mother lost her precious daughter Judith in stillbirth, she was able to empathize and comfort other mothers who had miscarried or lost their child. No one but one who has suffered the same sorrow can empathize with another. Jesus has that empathetic heart.

Third, the benefit of family adoption is in the third person of the Trinity: the Holy Spirit. As a member of the family of God, I have the indwelling of the Holy Spirit. Interestingly, Romans 8 refers to Him as the Spirit of *adoption*. As such, He bears witness of our salvation and adoption. He seals them forever. By that fact we have conviction of sin, assistance in understanding the Word, and completeness in Him. His Spirit indwelt in us at salvation gives us many gifts to enjoy in this age: "The fruit of the Spirit is love, joy, peace, longsuffering, gentleness, goodness, faith, meekness, temperance" (Galatians 5:22–23). Who would not want the legacy of love, joy, peace, etc.?

Fourth, a bequest of the inheritance in Christ is fellowship with others. All those who have accepted Christ's salvation have become brothers and sisters in Him—the enormous family of God. By such bequest and as a member of the family of God, I am never alone in this age. I have fellowship with other believers. That fellowship is unique in that I can recognize another family member without anyone ever formally introducing us.

Remember my friend Abby Shields, the one who handed out the "Who I Am in Christ" cards at a ladies' retreat? I became acquainted with

Abby at a public-school conference for teachers. God would use her keynote address to unite us together in friendship.

Standing at the back of the crowded room, I focused my full attention upon Abby's message. Our eyes momentarily met, and I suspected with that singular look that she was a Christian. Inspiring the group of teachers to stay the course, she went on to speak further about perfection not existing in a teacher, giving us all permission to mess up. She commented that there was only one perfect man, and we all knew what had happened to Him. Then she went on to speak about what she called, "Basic instructions before leaving earth," which was her way of injecting the Word into a secular education conference.

My assumptions about Abby proved to be true. She is a Christian, and because of that fact, we are sisters in Christ. Even though we had never met previously, once we met and talked at length, we became fast friends and remain so today.

As if all the previous benefits of salvation and our adoption were not enough, one day we will receive rewards as part of God's family.

Earthly benefactors will sometimes place inheritances in trust, whereby the recipient receives the inheritance when he or she reaches a certain age. The wealth builds as it remains in the trust account, but one day the vault will open, and the recipient will receive the legacy willed.

The inheritance the Christian possesses is also in trust, reserved in heaven. The Bible alludes to treasures that we children of God will receive at the judgment seat of Christ—gold, silver, and precious stones—an outcome of the service we have joyfully given for the Lord. In the meantime, they are laid up for us in trust with Christ in heaven. Only He will be worthy to present the awards to us in that day.

The legal community encourages everyone to have a will. Without one, our accumulated resources most often go to the state, leaving our loved ones bereft. Our children would miss the inheritance that they unwittingly have had a part in building. In loving consideration, parents typically bestow things of value to their children in their wills. For the Christian, the things of true value to bequeath ought to be the godly virtues proclaimed in God's Word. Christian parents will no doubt want their children to be a part of the family of God. They will also want to leave behind guiding principles and biblical instruction that will bode well for their children eternally.

God is no less intentional in His will. The admonition for all of us who stand in the shadow of His Son is to be witnesses for Christ to those who follow us: parents to their children, teachers to their students, and the church to the people the Holy Spirit places in our paths.

I've created a plan to distribute my valuables to loved ones when God calls me home. That plan protects my property and preserves my estate for the future. However, I have had a greater privilege that has heavenly rewards and is of great value to me. I have been privileged to lead some students, friends, and family members to the Lord through the work of the Holy Spirit and His Word. God has given me great opportunities to continue instruction to students who have graduated and are on their own life's journeys. They seek wisdom, and I am able, frail as I am, to provide biblical answers for them to some of life's most challenging questions. Furthermore, God has allowed me to be a trusted friend in valuable relationships.

I am thankful to God that I am able to leave a legacy to these loved ones—former students, friends, fellow believers, and my earthly family. An inheritance I received continues to impact others for Christ. Praise Him!

CHAPTER 25

Whatsoever Things Are True

MY GRANDPARENTS AND PARENTS REVERED THE TRUTH AND spoke the truth. They held two important beliefs: the truth of salvation and the truth of right thinking.

> Jesus saith until him, I am the way, the truth, and the life: no one cometh unto the Father, but by me. (John 14:6)

> For the word of God is quick, and powerful, and sharper than any twoedged sword, piercing even to the dividing asunder of soul and spirit . . . and is a discerner of the thoughts and intents of the heart. (Hebrews 4:12)

When I began teaching, I did not have the right thinking or the right vision of what kind of teacher I was to be. As I noted, my flawed progressive thinking led me to try to be a friend to my students. That progressivism led me to abject failure, largely because that sentiment reflected a false worldview instead of the truth. Only after being emmeshed in Christian education did I recognize the magnitude of responsible truth telling. Understanding the truth of God's Word (its doctrine) and applying it to my life (Christlikeness) come by direction and guidance of the Holy Spirit.

In order to understand and apply the Word, whom does the Holy Spirit guide me to follow? The answer is unequivocally the Master Teacher—Jesus Christ—who spoke with authority and practiced the Word He spoke. How could He do any less? He was the incarnate Word. With

Jesus Christ, the Master, as my guide, I sought to make a difference in my students' lives, especially in the public sector.

I would love to say that my fifty years of teaching were a string of masterful successes. While I have experienced some wonderful teaching moments and the fruit of those moments, I learned more truth from my failures than I did from my successes. One of the impactful truths I gleaned came as a result of a misdirected, legalistic mindset and, thus, an abject failure.

After a series of heartbreaking events in my life, I left Christian education for a while and began, once again, teaching in the public school. Subconsciously, my old legalistic set of expectations were back in force. Thankfully, in spite of my thinking, I learned an important lesson.

I stood at the door of the classroom, where I taught eighth-grade English, and welcomed my new students to class. The first student who grabbed my attention was Eddie, a clean-cut, well-groomed student, almost a carbon copy of the Christian school students who had graced my former classes. He had done his homework, for he knew my name and introduced himself at the door.

"Good morning, Miss Stewart. My name is Eddie. I can't wait to learn some English!"

"Well, good morning, Eddie. Thank you for introducing yourself. I am glad to have you in my class. I trust we will have an enjoyable time learning that English."

I knew with certainty Eddie would be one of my finest, most cooperative students.

Further down the line stood a taller young man, notable because of the fedora he wore on his head. When he reached my full view, I discovered this student had shoulder-length hair under that fedora, a long trench coat, and a confident baritone voice.

"Good morning," I said. "I am glad to see you this morning."

If I remember properly, his response was, "Right." And he moved on to take his seat.

I, with equal certainty, believed this young man was trouble with a capital T. I had carried over some of those preconceived, church-member preferences. I had judged two students based upon the cut of their hair and the appearance of their clothes.

You may have already guessed the outcome. Eddie, while looking the part of a well-behaved, manageable student, was rather the class clown and a thorn in my side, requiring patience and perseverance. Tim, the long-haired, trench-coat-donning student, was without a doubt one of the most gifted, polite, and intelligent young men it has been my privilege to teach.

I learned a masterful truth: Jesus accepted people just the way they came to Him without condemnation. Outward appearance may give a clue to thoughts and intents of a person's heart, but only truth is the reliable discerner of that heart.

I soon transitioned from junior high English to high school English. There I discovered the depth of intelligence and reasoning that many teenagers possess. Consequently, sometimes my students taught a better lesson than I did.

This lesson in telling the truth is memorable for two reasons: one, it was an example of appearance mimicking reality; and two, the lesson occurred on 9/11. On that fateful day, I had just begun my first hour of a sophomore English class. The intercom announced that all classroom teachers needed to have their TVs on. I remember wondering why, since we had already had the morning announcements over the TV in homeroom a short time ago. Nevertheless, I turned the TV on to view the horrible death and destruction and subsequent fall of the first Twin Tower.

In witnessing the implosion, one of students remarked, "Oh, why are we watching *Independence Day?*"

One of the other students responded, "Man! Shut up! I think this thing is real."

For his comment, he received my knowing teacher look, but the successive devastating events prevented me from addressing his comment further. We were to discover quickly how very real the event was.

After we had our worst fears confirmed, one of my students, Joey, spoke up, calmly and confidently. "Miss Stewart, I think we need to pray!"

Joey was one of my average students in a class of quite bright students who excelled in their studies. Yet he commanded the respect of the other students.

The student who had commanded that one student "shut up" now suggested Joey lead us. With my acknowledged permission, Joey led us in a prayer for the victims of this violence and our nation as a whole. He prayed that we would turn to God in this terrible time of evil. He also prayed for the enemies who had done this horrific thing.

Two valuable truths, among many, rang home to me that day. First, Joey was a peculiar student in my class and in the school; he stood out among others because he did not dress, walk, or talk like the rest. Students respected him because he was a Christian and modeled Christlikeness in his everyday walk. Joey held to the truth, "Love not the world, neither the things that are in the world. If any man love the world, the love of the Father is not in him" (1 John 2:15). Second, likenesses of reality often desensitize us so that when the real event happens we are numb to its significance.

My students and I stayed in class and watched the dreadful drama unfold: the second tower falling, a plane hitting the Pentagon, and brave passengers in Pennsylvania downing a plane, theorized as meant for the White House. We went home that evening to watch the events, which replayed over and over for days and weeks to come. I remember that the tears first shed that morning and throughout that day no longer creased my face on day two or three. I remember also that churches across the country, filled to capacity for a few weeks after that dreadful day, reverted back to commonplace reality, our independence from God reestablished.

It is true that God uses suffering to draw our hearts to Him. But often, once we have been delivered from the suffering, many of us initially thank God, only to forget the source of our deliverance, soon returning to our self-sufficient lives. Oh, that we would retain the truth of God alone as our deliverer!

I learned another lesson in presenting truth while teaching AP Language at Wilmington Christian Academy in North Carolina. Since I taught AP Language with its emphasis on nonfiction works, I knew the readings would present philosophies in direct contrast to the truth of the Word. I also knew that strong opinions often drown out truth, and respect for the opinions of others can easily evaporate during opinionated discussions. I wanted my students to understand that discerning the truth comes through the work of the Holy Spirit and the Word. I also wanted them to respect the rights of others to present their points of view.

My question became, "How can I present these philosophies in such a way that the students will respect but not accept the viewpoints of the false teachers?"

I chose a fun activity the first week of school to establish the practice of separating truth from error and titled the lesson, "What Do You See?" It contained several slides of negative-positive pictures. I showed the first slide and asked the students to tell me what they saw.

"I see an old woman!" one girl noted.

"What?!" another student spoke out. "It's a young woman."

"No way," another chimed in. "I don't see any women. I just see some blobs."

"I tell you, it's an old woman," the first girl countered.

I stopped the discourse to reveal that both an old woman and a young woman were present, depending upon one's point of view. I then outlined the curves of the faces of each woman.

The students exclaimed, "Now I see!"

I went on to show several contrasting images. Some students were right in their viewpoints; others were wrong, but each student had the opportunity to voice their opinions without attack by another.

"Class," I concluded., "in this study we are closely examining various authors' works that clearly do not reflect our beliefs. We must respect their right to those beliefs, but we must learn to counter their false ideas with biblical truth. Do you think you are ready for the challenge?"

"Yes," came the unanimous response.

In our study that year and years to follow, the students saw how close Plato in his *Republic* came to the truth but tragically did not see that the *Sun* of intellectualism's granting people wisdom was instead the *Son* of God, who is the source of true wisdom. We studied the *Humanist Manifestos I, II,* and *III* and unfortunately saw that humanistic philosophers have reached their agendas in ridding schools of the "archaic theology" that God created the earth and mankind. They have replaced the truth of creation with scientific "fact" known as evolution and have made science their god. They have convinced statesmen that a village raises a child, not the parents. My students became effective analyzers of the works and their philosophies, and thankfully they became counter claimers by using the Bible. Through the studies, students learned to sift everything through the Word of God, keeping what was wise and true and discarding what was man-centered and false.

Likewise, AP Literature afforded much discussion on philosophy as it pertains to humanity. Shakespeare, though not credited as a Christian, understood human nature. Through the characters of Macbeth, Julius Caesar, Hamlet, and King Lear, students saw the tragedy of man's thinking and its contrariness to the true thinking of Scripture. Students learned that unbridled ambition, revenge, and misguided definitions of love are destructive to one's life.

John Milton's *Paradise Lost* was the work my students most enjoyed picking apart. I paralleled that reading, of course, with Genesis 3. The discussion of these selections led to amazing conclusions.

"Miss Stewart." A student raised his hand. "I have read Genesis 3 a hundred times, and I never saw that Eve apparently lied to the serpent. She said, 'Ye shall not eat of the fruit of the tree . . . neither shall you touch it.' God commanded that they not eat of it. He didn't say they would die if they touched it."

"That's right. Good observation," I responded.

Ashley noted, "Eve gets the blame for the fall, but the Scripture says that Adam stood close by. Then he had to know what the serpent was up to."

"Good observation. What did you pull from the serpent's discourse with Eve in *Paradise Lost*?" I asked.

"Satan mixed truth and error!" Abby stated.

"How so?" I queried.

"He suggested that animals ate of the fruit and did not die. He stated that death was no threat, for they didn't know what death was. He boasted that God did not want them to have the knowledge because then they would be gods. True, they had not experienced death; they died spiritually but not physically. God didn't want them to eat of the fruit because the knowledge would bring death. He wanted them to obey Him though. We don't know but can surmise that animals did eat of the fruit. Truth and error together."

"I saw that the fruit appealed to Eve's lusts," Paige added. "The lust of the eyes, the lust of the flesh, and the pride of life."

After much discussion, we drew yet another conclusion regarding truth. The world will tempt us in our lusts and draw us away from the truth. Evil looks pretty like the fruit, but underneath is destruction. The world's philosophies mix just enough truth with error to trap the non-so-ber-minded thinker. We can lie to God and ourselves by believing we know better than He about how we should live our lives and what wisdom we should follow.

We concluded the lesson with: "Whatsoever things are of good report . . . think on these things" (Philippians 4:8).

There were many lessons about truth embedded in my English classes. For example: (1) How we handle the Word of God is how we would handle seeing Jesus face to face. (2) Even though Christians are separated from the world, we have often moved in the position vacated by worldly views, as they moved further left. (3) I have declared, I love you, Lord, with all my heart, soul, mind, and strength when I have, in reality, sectioned off portions of my heart that I refused to relinquish to God.

On occasion, I used science to teach a truth lesson in Bible class. I met one day with a student who had lost her mother and carried bitterness toward God and others. She was so overcome with grief and bitterness that she had shut God out.

Having lost both my mom and dad, I empathized with her but could not entirely do so, for she had been a preteen when her mother died. I so wanted to relieve her distress that I made the error of going between her and God with my advice. Confronting the source of her bitterness, as I had suggested, did not turn out well. My error was twofold: not praying before offering the advice and stepping in between God's working and His child.

God, all by Himself, did a miraculous transformation in this then teenage girl. With her permission, I shared my failures with my Bible class.

"Girls, I want to share with you a terrible mistake I made. I tried to fix a sad situation in someone's life without allowing God to use the situation to mold and make this young lady into what He desired. I went ahead of Him, and the mistake was costly."

"I am sure you are all familiar with the butterfly and how it begins as a caterpillar, forms a chrysalis, and emerges as a beautiful butterfly. Mistakenly, people have tried to help the butterfly in its struggle for freedom by cutting the chrysalis away. The butterfly, unfortunately, cannot then develop, and it dies. The struggle to rid itself of the chrysalis is what develops the butterfly's wings and gives it strength to fly. I cut the chrysalis of this girl's struggle, but God intervened and did the work in her. I made the mistake of interfering in God's business."

I ended the lesson by encouraging my students with the admonitions of Philippians 4:8: "Whatsoever things are true . . . lovely . . . think on these things."

As a teacher, I have the responsibility of presenting content in a way that students understand. It's important that my method of presenting the truth is given with authority. I measure the success of my teaching by my students' retention of the content. A movie I saw recently reminded me of the dynamic. A dog had an encounter with a skunk, and it sprayed her. The dog's caretaker then came in contact with the dog, which, of course, caused them both to stink. In reverse, if I as a caretaker fail, my students will fail.

When teaching AP classes, I define the word *philosophy* in this manner: a system of beliefs that drives our actions. People often refer to philosophy today as one's worldview. All of us, not just teachers, have a philosophy or worldview—things we believe that compel us to do what we do. Just as the skunk impacted the dog, what we do impacts others. Our beliefs determine what we do, so our beliefs also impact others.

I am a teacher by profession, but I have come to realize that *all* individuals are teachers whether they recognize it or not. We teach by our walk—our actions—and by what we deliberate in our minds—our beliefs. Truth thinking and truth telling are imperative to a walk of Christlikeness and to a godly heritage.

CHAPTER 26

Is Our Legacy for the Next Generation a Biblical One?

SHADOWS ARE EPHEMERAL THINGS. IF PEOPLE OR OBJECTS STAND directly in the way of the sun, they cast solid silhouettes on the ground that someone may easily stand in. Shadows can also be flitting, as specks of sunlight peek through fingers, leaves of trees, or architectural designs to cast quivering, incomplete images. Such shadows, providing only a distorted image of the person or thing casting the shadow, are difficult to capture and to walk therein. The sun may even move behind a cloud or its rays move behind an object and block the light; then, we may catch only a glimpse of a shadow before it is gone.

Why do I speak of flitting shadows? Why do I recount family stories that affirm a trust in God and describe the shadows that impacted my life? Why do I speak of a godly heritage? Why do I bring us together at this juncture? My answer is *fear*.

In chapter one, I asked the question, "What are we afraid of?" The answer was that we may have failed to do our job of casting the right shadows for the next generations. I fear that they would not see Jesus in us. I cannot help but fear that my own generation has led the coming generations to be like God's chosen people of the Old Testament . . . wandering in the wilderness, complaining, demanding, rebelling, and dying without God. I fear that like in the days of Sodom and Gomorrah, God, in the not-too-distant future, may not be able to find ten faithful ones upon the earth. I fear that time is exceedingly short to teach the next generations to trust in, to stand for, and to speak out about the gospel.

I personally fear that what I have failed to do will impact my students negatively and will leave them without the godly heritage I possessed and had planned to bequeath to them. Quite succinctly, I fear those flitting shadows.

I have had a platform from which to observe the generations since my own. I have apologized to my classes for the shameful actions of my generation. After five decades of educational experience, I can attest that while culture in the United States has radically changed, the needs of students have not. They still require someone to love them unconditionally; someone to love them enough to say no, thereby establishing clear and protective boundaries; and someone to challenge them to do their best, especially in service to God. While they may outwardly rebel at the rules in place for their safety and instruction, or even rebuff offered love, they internally recognize and appreciate the presence of love and secure boundaries. I would suggest that all human beings, not just young people, have a basic need to know that they matter—that they are loved by someone—and they, like children, will sometimes resort to drastic measures to secure that affection.

Serving as principal in a Christian school in North Carolina, I was chief disciplinarian, among other duties. When a teacher felt management needed reinforcement, she would send the offending child to me.

One fourth-grade boy was a regular visitor to my office. His early home life had been tumultuous, and he had come to live with his grandparents. His grandmother was a godly woman who insisted that her grandson be a student in the school. The grandfather, unfortunately, was not a godly influence. The duplicity of that environment and past history crushed that student. He was starved for the right attention, but he only knew how to attract negative attention, which routinely resulted in visits with his principal.

"Chuck, what did you do?" I refrained from the words *this time*. I didn't want to highlight the number of past visits, always hoping that this one might be the last.

"I shoved Michael," he answered.

"Why did you shove Michael?" I continued with routine questioning.

"He had my place in line! He knows it's my place."

"I see. And what should you have done?" I suspected he knew the right answer.

"I should have let him have my place."

"Chuck, you know because I love you, I cannot allow you to get by with this. What am I going to do?"

"Spank me?" he questioned. We had been at this spot before; because of his frequent visits, he was due for a reckoning.

I paddled Chuck enough to hurt his pride but not enough to harm his body. The accompanying tears ensued, but then Chuck did something he had never done before . . . he threw his arms around me.

Stunned and returning his hug, I asked, "Why the hug, Chuck?"

"Because you *love* me, and I *love* you!"

Realization sunk in. His teacher and I had cared enough about this boy that we had said no.

I walked Chuck to his classroom. His teacher met me at the door with a poignant look.

"Miss Stewart, I can always see the wheels of Chuck's thinking turning before he acts up. It's like he is plotting what he can do to be sent to the office."

"I believe I know the reason." I shared my concern, along with a summary of the previous event. "Let's try something. The next time you see those wheels turning, send Chuck to the office before he acts. Linda (my secretary) or I will talk with him and assure him of our love. Let's see what happens."

Chuck came on regular occasions for a few weeks. Sometimes he was so angry, he wanted to hit someone, so he hit my couch cushion instead. Other times, we talked calmly through his thoughts. Soon Chuck no longer needed to make the trips; he had accepted that we loved him without his needing to act out for attention. Today the *village philosophy* would not sanction our discipline plan or the hug we shared.

If students' needs have not changed, then what has changed about the shadows? Clearly from my realm of observation, our culture has rejected absolute truth—the truth found only in God's Word. People have exchanged the absolute truth of Scripture for the relative truth of the world. This exchange has become increasingly obvious even in the Christian realm.

In my girls' Bible classes, I held a question-and-answer Friday once a month. The girls would circle the "wagons" (chairs), and we would discuss whatever topics or issues they wished to address. They would typically submit their questions on Monday, giving me the opportunity to prepare the answers based upon the Word. I became increasingly stunned by the topics and thinking that accompanied those topics. Sometimes questions arose out of the discussion that I had not prepared for, but the truth of Scripture remained my guide.

"Ms. Stewart, do you think it is all right for a couple to live together before marriage?" began a questioner after I had answered a question on the biblical view of marriage.

"No, I don't," I responded.

As I proceeded to answer the question further, another student interrupted, "But what if they plan on marrying? Isn't it a smart idea to see if they can live together before they marry? Isn't that better than marrying and then divorcing?"

"What does the Bible say about sex before marriage?" I asked.

"I know; it's forbidden. But what if sex is not involved? What if the couple just wants to see how well they fit together?"

"Well, first, the best way to see if you fit is spending time together in God's Word. Time spent in genuine conversation about your views, likes, and dislikes is also helpful. Spending time with his family shows you how he treats his mother and how he would probably treat you. All these things will help you know him better without living together."

"My sister lives with a guy, but they only do that to help with finances while in college," another student interjected. "What is wrong with that?"

"Regardless of the reasons, your sister and her friend are giving the appearance of evil" (1 Thessalonians 5:22).

"Appearance of evil? How can people know what is going on inside the apartment? What business is it of theirs anyway?" she pushed.

"They probably can't. But your sister is suggesting by her cohabitation that something is going on. Would you judge me if I shared my home with a male teacher?"

"Yes!" the girls unanimously answered.

"Why is it okay for your sister but not for me?"

"You're a teacher!" one girl exclaimed adamantly.

"And I am a Christian, just like most of you. I have a responsibility to honor Christ's name by my actions. Even if the arrangement were merely for financial assistance, I would give the appearance of wrongdoing."

Almost all of the girls agreed with my answer, and we moved on.

Other later discussions, however, affirmed that several of the girls had bought into the world's relative, circumstantial truth. They might agree with the basic concepts of biblical worldview but hedge on absolute truth; hence, they may compromise truth at any given moment.

For example, they may believe that under some circumstances, abortion is permissible or that lying is acceptable. And because the government is corrupt, they may believe that under some circumstances, cheating is acceptable. Truth, for them, is relative to the circumstances rather than to absolutes.

Another major change over the last fifty years is the erosion of authority in society. People who have authoritative rule—the president, Congress, law enforcement officers, judges, principals, teachers, parents, etc.—suffer belittlement, abuse, and even threats to their lives instead of the respect their positions once held. Some treatment has forced outstanding teachers, police officers, and elected officials to abandon their careers. Why is this blatant disregard for authority important to the Christian? The answer should be obvious to us: *how we respond to earthly authority is how we respond to God's authority.* After all, if I can remove all authority, especially God's, I am free to do as I please. In today's culture we have exchanged God's authority for self-rule.

Right or wrong, the view of a teacher or principal in my early days of teaching was that the teacher was right until proven wrong. I can share here a still painful example from my own schooling.

I needed an elective in high school, and since I was planning on being a teacher, I chose personal typing. I thought the class would be a piece of cake, but learning the keyboard, developing speed, and typing without errors became the bane of my existence.

Nevertheless, this type A personality dug in. I improved and arrived at the point of the final exam: to type a written passage without error or erasures. The teacher who shall remain nameless declared that any erasures would mean an F on the exam. I began the grueling task and was able, surprisingly, to type without error. I removed my very excellent manuscript from the typewriter and placed it aside. I covered the typewriter, which, too, was a command from said teacher.

In the meantime, a fellow student laid his pencil down on my paper—an innocent action—but the pencil left a small pencil mark. Unthinking, I took the pencil and erased the offending mark and walked to the teacher to turn in my perfect A paper.

The teacher scanned the document and held the paper up to the light. He declared in a loud voice, "Erasure—F!"

I was mortified, and I do have to admit, I protested. He listened to both me and the offending owner of the pencil, but the grade still stood. My final grade was a B-, an offensive grade to a type A student.

When I arrived home that evening, my father's usual question awaited me: What had I learned in school? I told him that I had learned that Mr. _____ was terribly mean and unfair. Seeking sympathy and hopefully intervention to correct the grievous error, I told Dad the story.

His response was, "Did you or did you not have an erasure?" (Absolute truth)

I replied, "I did, but—"

"Then the matter is settled." (Absolute Respect for Authority)

We were done, and my grade still stands. My father's belief was that the teacher was the authority in the right. That view of authority is rare today. While some authorities in their humanity make mistakes, more often than not, authority is right in its judgment.

In our culture we have witnessed the absence of authority in rioting, shootings, grab-and-go robberies, and open ridicule of authorities in our

White House and congressional halls. Even in our churches, we Christians have offensively attacked those in authority who do not believe the same as we do. Though we are to stand for truth, we are not to offend in the same manner or worse than those we oppose. We are to "love [our] enemies and pray for those who persecute [us]" (Matthew 5:44 ESV). Are we Christians showing a disrespect for God's authority, which He has placed over us? Are we casting a shadow of offense in front of the next generations?

Only slightly different is erosion of the authority in the home. The father is to be the head of the home as Christ is the head of the church. We have rejected the Christlike position in exchange for equal rights among all family members, especially the children. It has become all too common for fathers to abandon their families. And in many other homes, fathers abandon their positions. Being a schoolteacher, I have seen this fact played out in parent conferences over the years.

For instance, I was new to a Christian school, and even though I had been teaching for more than thirty years, I found the new experience challenging. Teachers had warned me that students would give any new teacher a trial by fire. While I was met with slight resistance, I soon had a good rapport with students. What surprised me was the parental advocacy—seeking preferential treatment for their teenage darlings. One conference remains firmly entrenched in my memory.

The mother and father met with me regarding their tenth-grade son's essay grade. The mother took charge of the conference, and the father was silent.

"Kevin feels that you graded his essay too severely," the mother began.

"What was the problem—content or structure that upset him?"

"Both. Why did you cut his grade so drastically over grammar?"

"Because he had too many serious grammar errors. He did have an opportunity to correct those for his final draft, but he submitted his essay without revision."

"But he had some good points," she protested.

"Yes, he did, but he didn't support them."

"He still should not have had a D on this essay!" she retorted.

After several back-and-forth comments, I interjected, "Mrs. _____, I am not your son's enemy. I am here to help him grow in his writing and to prepare him for his future, whether it is college or the work force."

"Well, you are certainly not being very encouraging toward that end!"

In desperation and without forethought, I said, "What is it you want, Mrs. _____?"

"I think he should have a B."

Gambling on her possible response, I opened my gradebook and readied my pencil. "All right, I will mark a B, but both you and I know he did not earn it."

"I don't want you to do that!"

"You don't? Then are you okay with my continuing to help your son do his best?"

"I suppose, but I will be watching his grades and you, Ms. Stewart!"

We parted on civil terms even though I lived under that threat for a while. Notably, during the entire conference, the father never said a word and merely nodded as he left the room. His position was the authority, but his wife had usurped that authority. In her desire for good grades for her son, she had put desire over integrity. She wanted her son to be happy with an unearned grade, not with his best.

Early on in my career, Christian parents desired for their children to have solid, biblical values, to be good citizens with a sense of pride in and ownership of their country, and to possess a strong work ethic that would build for them a home and family. Even if the parents were not Christians, they still strove to be good people. From these goals came a respect for others' rights and privileges and a recognition of and obedience to authorities. It also resulted in communities that interacted with each other in neighborhood settings. To help secure such wishes, many parents enrolled their children in Christian schools.

These schools, as a response to the societal shifts of the sixties, offered parents and students assistance in biblical instruction, in addition to academic curriculum. God was at the center of spiritual, academic, social, and physical growth. Instruction countered the evolutionary theory, secular humanism, and lifestyle living contrary to the Word of God. Parents and students in those schools explored God-centered careers: missions work, the pastorate, other full-time Christian service, or positions in the secular workplace with a determination to witness for Christ. Students examined the gifts the Holy Spirit had bequeathed to them at salvation and assessed how they could best use those gifts for ministry. Biblical instruction began in kindergarten and continued, for many, beyond high school to a Christian college or university. The parents believed this plan secured God's best for their children.

Today parents, for the most part, do love their children and seek the best for them, but the definition of *best* has changed significantly and dramatically. Largely, their goals for their children have a different focus than years ago when Christian schools began.

As an example, a Christian schoolteacher friend of mine recently met with his students' parents, most of whom profess to be Christians. He asked parents what they wanted for their children's future. The answer was overwhelmingly the same: happiness. Now, initially that answer would seem harmless since the word *happiness* is such a regular part of our vernacular. The reality, however, is that the answer is quite telling and the thinking quite perilous. What do you suppose these parents believe would bring about that happiness? Although he did not further question the parents for their answers, I would guess that their definition of happiness would have something to do with success measured by an accumulation of money.

Today most professing Christians consider a career pathway that will garner the most money in a secular job and a home in a pleasurable, secular community.

In response you might ask, is God against money and success? Is it a sin to be rich? The answer to those questions is no. God abundantly blessed notable biblical saints: Abraham, Job, David, Solomon, Lydia, Dorcas, and Joseph of Arimathea, to name a few, so God does not oppose financial success. What is crucial is the heart motive of these saints.

Abraham allowed his nephew Lot to have the well-watered, bountiful plain, yet Abraham, for his generosity, prospered more than Lot. Job lost all to show his allegiance to God, and God restored in greater abundance. David and Solomon, although the wealthiest of their day, both testified to the vanity of great riches. Lydia and Dorcas used their finances to support the apostles. Joseph provided an expensive tomb for the body of Jesus. Money was not the driving force in their lives . . . God was. First Timothy 6:17 (ESV) affirms God's admonition: "As for the rich in this present age, charge them not to be haughty, nor to set their hopes on the *uncertainty of riches*, but on God, who richly provides us with everything to *enjoy*" (emphasis added by author).

What should always be the determination of our life plans? The answer is clear: to set as a daily goal to love the Lord God and to be Christlike by trusting and obeying His Word. He says so in John 14:15 (ESV): "If you love me, you will keep my commandments." Consequently, since our children are a heritage from a loving God, should we not approach Him regarding His will for ourselves and for them?

Ridding ourselves of absolute truth and a proper respect for authority has led us to self-focus, looking to ourselves for all of life's answers.

As an only child, I could have become quite spoiled, but my parents never allowed that! I earned my own money beginning at age fifteen, and I learned the value of working to buy what I needed and sometimes wanted. One thing, however, destroyed my aspiration to manage my money well: credit. Since I worked for Montgomery Ward while a teenager, they gave me a credit account—yes, as a sixteen-year-old. I could buy things without money in hand and pay for them in installments. I had the false sense that those things bought on credit were mine. The credit card entitled me, but in reality, the company still owned the items. (By the way, they cost me far more than if I had paid for them with money in hand.) Later in my early twenties, I bought my first car through the bank where I worked. I mistakenly believed the car belonged to me at the outset. I, however, did not own the car until I paid the debt and had the title in hand. Then, and only then, did the word *entitlement* have significance.

When I began my teaching career, the teacher's union went on strike. I spent the first days of my educational career on the picket line, to my father's chagrin. (He had fought in WWII for my right to protest against the educational system, and he believed that protest to be a travesty.) I didn't understand everything about the political aspect of education at that time, so I followed the actions of *experienced* teachers. Their view, unlike my dad's, declared that I had rights that needed to be respected. Rights, even then, became a central focus.

Thus, today I have observed the overstated demand for one's democracy-sanctioned rights and the entitlement that accompanies those rights. These rights have caused people, even Christians, to reject a higher power: to exchange the dictates of a majority for self-government. To act in this way is to be self-centered. To have such a self-focus takes our eyes off the shadows we are casting for the next generation. Consequently, our children, too, have become self-focused and entitled. Self-centeredness is synonymous with selfishness, and selfishness left unchecked turns to wanting what I want, however I want it . . . and preferably without paying for it with cash in hand. Selfishness left unchecked is greed.

A definition of *greed* or *avarice* found in the ever-popular *Wikipedia* is an "inordinate or insatiable longing for material gain, be it food, money, status, or power. As a secular psychological concept, greed is an inordinate desire to acquire or possess *more than one needs*."[3]

Greed, consequently, goes beyond one's need. To pursue wants beyond needs, and especially one's means, is self-indulgence. According to Philippians 4:19, God promises to supply all our needs, not our wants. While buying something we want in and of itself is not sinful, constant spending to our wants takes our hearts' focus off others, especially God, and places it upon ourselves.

A key word in this definition is *insatiable*; a synonym would be voracious. What image do you have when you hear the word *voracious*? You might see a rapacious animal like the wolf or a tiger; however, one of the most voracious of all animals is swine, better known as the pig or hog.

As noted often, I began life on a farm, and I lived there until almost ten. One of my chores was to go with Mom or Dad, or later, when old enough, by myself to slop the hogs.

Hogs are interesting, perhaps to some even disgusting animals. Swine normally don't associate with humans unless they are bearing food. Then they run, regardless of size, to the slop troughs. Once the solid and liquid mixture lands in the troughs, they dive in, sometimes literally. They grunt as they eat and nose out every morsel until no food remains. Hogs rarely care what the slop contains. They are only concerned that their bellies will be filled. After eating, they grunt, roll in the mud, or scratch their backs on fence rails or posts. To them that is the happy life. Do you think they are content? No. If you approach the pig pen after feeding, they will run again as fast as they can, expecting to be fed even though they have just eaten.

The point is that greed—the self-indulgent pursuit of happiness—can never be satisfied. If we, as Christians, then pursue happiness, we, too, will never be satisfied.

Paul said in Philippians 4:11, "Not that I speak in respect of want, for I have learned in whatsoever state I am therewith to be content." Contentedness is the goal of the Christian, not happiness.

David said in Psalm 37:4, "Delight thyself also in the LORD, and he shall give thee the desires of thine heart." I remember as I child, I thought this verse meant I could have *anything I wanted*; however, as I grew older and more mature in the faith, I came to understand that as I spend intimate, personal time with the Lord in His Word, my desires would line up with His desires. Crucial to attaining these desires is that intimate, personal relationship with Him. To neglect that relationship is to relinquish His best and to replace it with my personal pursuit—my greedy desire.

Happiness is fickle; it depends upon circumstances (now accepted as a probable foundation for truth). People may be happy today because the sun is shining, they feel well physically, and all is right with the world. Happiness, though, rarely delivers for any extended period. A new home may bring happiness until a water leak damages a sizable portion, it begins to show its age, or the family outgrows it. A new car may bring happiness until someone scratches the finish, it breaks down, or it begins to show its age. A large bankroll may provide the illusion of happiness until taxes come due, property insurance increases exorbitantly, or overextended credit card bills arrive. Thus, happiness is one of those flickering shadows. If the pursuit of happiness is mercurial, why would we so adamantly pursue that which fluctuates from day to day?

As a result of our self-focus, other troublesome concerns arise.

For example, *selfies* are properly named. The name depicts our desire to capture the best, often staged, appearance of ourselves or to post a perfect environment—a false presentation of who we are and where we live. In scriptural terms that would be *hypocrisy*. Technology, while not the cause of flitting shadows, has contributed to our self-focus. What did we ever do without the cell phone?

I was shopping recently in a large antiques mall. I temporarily lost contact with my cousin. Instead of getting more exercise by walking up and down the aisles, as I would have done prior to today's technology, I called her on the phone.

"Where are you?" I queried.

"Aisle six," she answered, and I made my way to connect with her. Only then did we connect face to face.

Technology and forward thinking would seem to give us more personal connections; however, Facebook, Snapchat, and Twitter, although presented as such, give us a false sense of friendships and personal interaction. I have a family member who boasts she has 962 friends; she does not. She has 962 Facebook contacts.

Additionally, we post or text instead of talking on the phone, visiting, sending cards, or drafting a snail-mail letter. Increasingly, people, even Christians, seem to have retreated into the technological world of fewer interpersonal relationships. Could it be possible, then, that as we connect less with others, we might connect even less with God?

Oftentimes, a drastic circumstance, like a violent storm, a pandemic, or devastating fires, causes us to recognize the need for community collaboration and rescue. We unite to shoulder the catastrophe together. We even fill the church pews or unite in a prayer vigil. Then, sadly, when the crisis is over or averted, we retreat from the community and back to our self-focused pursuits. Could God be using such means to open our eyes to those around us? Could He be directing through these catastrophes an intercommunication with Him? Could He be asking us to look to the Light of His presence? These are questions worth asking.

Another observed outgrowth of this self-focus is instant gratification—receiving what we want when we want it has made us and our children impatient, complaining, and discontented individuals. We become cranky if the internet is a nanosecond slow, if we must wait in line at the store or even the self-check-out stations. If the traffic is not moving at our desired speed, we may use our horns, talk offensively to the drivers (behind closed windows), or make some gesture that may or may not be misunderstood—all in the name of our personal inconvenience. Could our children or others be watching and hearing our displeasure?

I have observed that in the pursuit of happiness, we also focus on comfort. At times, we will go to any lengths and pay any price for comfort. Now, I do understand that no one invites pain; that would be psychologically disturbing. However, we do run to anything that will alleviate our discomfort. Our toleration of discomfort is a subtle invader in the church as well. We want comfortable clothing, comfortable seating, and comfortable messages that aren't too long and that appeal to the ear but don't interfere with our daily lives. I wonder if I or anyone I know could hold up under the discomfort of the Depression or the oppression of an anti-God regime like Hitler's Holocaust. Yet older generations did, and Christians in other countries still do.

Could even our posture and comfort in worship say anything about us? It might express pride or humility. A little discomfort—like kneeling on our knees in a hay mow—might just be the humility we need in response to an awesome, loving, and just God. Are we teaching our children to forgo the discomfort of God's instruction and discipline so that they remain comfortable? Are we leaving that kind of heritage?

My former pastor, J. D. Herchehahn, had the uncanny ability to assure me while in his presence that I mattered to him. He always gave me his undivided attention and responded to me with that assuring, cheerful smile. He often talked and sang from the pulpit about JOY—*J*esus, *O*thers, and *Y*ou. He radiated joy. Today, I am afraid we have succumbed to *YOJ*!

Joy, rather than happiness, is a biblical gift. The Holy Spirit endows the Christian with joy at salvation. God in His sovereignty desires for His children to possess the ever-fixed joy—joy that does not alter or flit. In contrast to happy, joy, as described in Scripture, may result from diverse and difficult circumstances. James 1:2–3 says, "My brethren, count it all *joy* when ye fall into divers temptations; knowing this, that the trying of your faith worketh patience" (emphasis added by author). The Christian can trust that difficulties in life will bring about godly results—a joy that assures that God strengthens, instructs, and matures the Christian through the trial.

Having difficulties in life is far more believable than the rosy-colored happy days. Consequently, joy is a far greater possession than happiness. Jesus Christ does not change as the world changes. He is "the same yesterday, and to day, and for ever" (Hebrews 13:8). The triune God is not fickle; neither is joy. God does not produce fleeting shadows as the world does.

Are our shadows becoming disintegrated, flitting, and difficult to see, let alone stand in? By our actions is it possible that we have taught our children to demand what they "need" immediately, if not sooner? As we pursue the "good life" of happiness, do we want it in order to serve God, or do we want the "good life" apart from God? Have we taken a twisted, deistic, genie-in-the-bottle view of God and His authority that demands, "Don't interfere with my personal affairs until I need you; then please fulfill my wishes immediately"? These are viable questions.

One of my colleagues in graduate school commented one day that in teaching we should model what we expect. Here, I trust, is an eye-opening example for us all.

In the late sixties a public service announcement showed a man relaxing underneath a tree and drawing on a cigarette. The camera zoomed out to show a young boy seated beside him, his fingers poised as if drawing on a cigarette as well. The caption read, "Like father, like son."

We—all Christians, not just parents—must model what we expect. If we expect people to follow the teachings of God's Word and to be ambassadors for Him, we must set that model before them: we must be the example in action, not just words. True, we are not perfect, but we can—no, we must—have the right biblical expectations and make sure we are living out those expectations before our present and the younger generations. We must cast a shadow that comes from the Light of God. We must make God so real in our lives that others will desire to walk in our shadows. We must amass a legacy of biblical truth, obedience to God's authority, and a Christ-centered life to leave as an inheritance. So I ask, my friends, how are we doing? I fear not so well. The good news, however, is that "perfect love casteth out fear" (1 John 4:18).

CHAPTER 27

Is It Too Late to Cast a Christlike Shadow?

NOW THAT I AM OF RETIREMENT AGE, HARDLY A DAY GOES BY THAT I do not receive email or snail mail reminders to make or adjust retirement decisions. Some less than reassuring announcements suggest that if I have not accumulated X amount of dollars, I will not be able to survive. Countless advertisements on TV and in magazines from Charles Schwab, E*Trade, and the like admonish me that I should have saved more when I was younger, but it is never too late to begin. Assessing one's financial future is good planning.

Assessing one's past spiritual influence and planning for the future is far more important. The current problematic situation is that we have failed to provide *solid, unwavering* shadows of Christlikeness for those who will follow. We may have succeeded in some areas, but as a body of believers, we have often succumbed to promoting our own self-interests over God and others. We have considered our futures, but we may not have adequately considered the futures of those under our influence.

Examining how we have lived our lives before others and then pronouncing ourselves guilty before God is thankfully not the end of the matter. Just as it is never too late to take financial responsibility, it is never too late to change direction—to make a repentant 180-degree turn. One of the many amazing things about our Lord and Savior Jesus Christ is that He does not condemn us. He forgives us when we come to Him in absolute humility and agree with Him about the sinful focus of our lives (1 John 1:9). He declares that there is now no condemnation for us (Romans 8:1).

Furthermore, Jesus Christ understands the temptations of this world—the lust of the flesh, the lust of the eyes, and the pride of life—because Satan tempted Him with the same offerings. And that temptation came in Christ's physical weakness, after forty days in the wilderness without nourishment and rest (Matthew 4:1–11). Since He so clearly knows our flesh, because He created it, He has an incomprehensible measure of grace to meet that repentant need. At the cross He provided the forgiveness of sin—past, present, and future. Once we have confessed our failures, we are free as "the light of the world" to cast the right shadows.

When teaching essay or speech writing, I instruct students to flesh out the problem, then observe, analyze, advance various solutions, and draw the most effective conclusion that issues a challenge to action. I am at that point in this book. I *encourage* you to begin now to adjust or build that legacy you wish to leave behind. Although my grandparents, parents, and I were not or are not perfect, we all desired to follow the One who is. I am sure you desire the same, so let's talk about this crucial shift in our thinking and actions.

Beyond repentance (godly sorrow) for our sin, how do we address the harms that we have done to others? The answer is parallel to the confession to God: it is an open and honest confession to our children or people in our circle of influence. Allow me, once again, to use a classroom example, for that is the area I know best.

Classroom management is one of the hardest things a teacher must tackle, for no course truly prepares one for the trenches. Management comes with experience. Nevertheless, college instructors try to assist the best they can. For instance, they would laughingly tell us young recruits not to smile until Thanksgiving. They instructed us to start firmly, saying that we could always lighten up but never gain ground lost to commencing too easily. I, foolishly, did not always adhere to the no-smiling-until-Thanksgiving precept. Allow me to share my foolishness and the blessed restoration that followed.

I had returned to public school after a few years in Christian education, and I was having trouble with one of my all-time best classes. Because I saw great promise in those students, I had made a grave error; I had been too easy on them discipline-wise. I shared my concern with a Christian friend and colleague. She suggested that I own up to my error and restore a firm but loving atmosphere in the classroom. I could, despite violating the professorial dictate, restore order and firmness. The next Monday's class went something like this:

"Good morning, class. Before we begin today's work, I want to apologize to all of you. I have made a grave mistake."

With that introduction, I had the students' rapt attention. Some even leaned further in to hear the confession, though I doubted they expected what was to come.

"I began this year being too lenient with you. You need boundaries just like the guidelines I have instituted in other classes. Because I saw you as a class with much promise, I allowed you some freedoms I should not have. Because I love you and want you to be the best you can be, I am from this day forward establishing the following guidelines."

I went on to set the boundaries for the class. Their response was surprisingly straightforward; they loved it. While they outwardly had been relishing the laxity, they were inwardly floundering in the permissive atmosphere. Order and expectations firmly established my authority and gave them freedom to surrender the authority that was not theirs to own. We had a phenomenally successful year, and that class will forever be one of my fondest and most treasured classes.

Why would I share this story with you? Simply because I am a flawed human being. I do not have all the answers. Sometimes I just need *hope*. I often *hope* my students know by my actions that I love them; even though I tell them regularly, I want my actions to match my speech. I also *hope* I do not say something stupid, and worse yet, don't recognize that I have. (Sarcasm is an easy humor to implement, but it can be hurtful if directed toward a student, especially in a crowd.) I often *hope* they will forgive my weaknesses just as Christ does. I *hope* my students learn the life lessons as much as they learn the language arts lessons. I *hope* that students will see a difference in me and desire to know about it. (We are, after all, called to be a peculiar people; Christians are to stand out for the right reasons—because we are modeling Christ.) I continue in *hope* to be a Christlike influence. I find my *hope* in Jesus Christ.

I *encourage* you in *hope*; a sinful flaw is rectified when a Christian comes clean with others. We can then begin adhering to the authority of biblical instruction.

I find I am most flawed when I have lost sight of my awe of God and have viewed myself as good and righteous. Often, God through His word shows me His might and power, His majesty and glory, His worthiness of my devotion. "As it is written, there is none righteous, no, not one." (Romans 3:10) After coming clean with Him about my idolatrous heart, I seek, once again, to walk in His ways, to trust and obey His word, and, thus, live for Him in Christlikeness.

I *encourage* you to ask key questions: are you in awe of God? Or are you more in awe of your own abilities, intelligence, position, or power? Are you more in awe of what the world has to offer you than your eternal destiny with God? The first step to showing an awesome God to others is to be in awe of Him ourselves. The knowledge of His awesomeness comes through His Word; therefore, we must be in His word.

I *encourage* you to be daily in His word, not just on Sunday or sporadically through the week but daily. Personal time spent in God's Word is foundational to one's own maturity in the faith. (It is interesting that the practice is called a devotional, for at its core is devotion to Him.) To mature their faith and yours, I *encourage* you to have a dedicated time of sharing God's Word with the family or with a circle of friends or church members. If we do not instruct our children in the Word, someone else will. What faith do you desire for them to have—biblical or worldly?

My family did not have a devotional time together except at Christmas and Easter. Dad always read the Christmas story from Luke 2 on Christmas Eve. Then we would sing Christmas carols together, ending with "Silent Night." At Easter, he would recount the walk up Calvary's hill, the crucifixion, and the resurrection. I wish we had met together regularly, not necessarily every day but often. Regardless, I knew from their lives they had personal meetings with God in the Scriptures.

I *encourage* you to have a personal prayer time; after devotions is a good time for such practice. Prayer is our communication with God, and the interpersonal conversing with Him about His word strengthens our faith. A vertical relationship with God makes horizontal relationships with others function more effectively. Prayer is also an interceding on behalf of those we love or a country we love. Prayer directs our thoughts toward God and others.

I *encourage* you to have a family prayer time or prayer circle with friends. Prayer times allow others to see our struggles and our needs which they may also have. To reveal our frailties humbles us and may embolden others to share their struggles as well. What are we afraid will happen if we share with the family (either our own family members or members of the family of God) our spiritual weaknesses and dependency upon God to meet our needs? What a blessing it is to praise God for answered prayer! How else will others see the results of prayer if they have not been privy to our requests?

Prayer warrior is a familiar term from my childhood. Many in my local country church had the reputation of being that kind of saint. These believers would spend hours in prayer over the names of the lost. While they prayed for the physical needs of church members and their families, the greater portion of their prayer focus was on the souls of loved ones or even strangers (a rock house mentality like my grandfather's). These people lived out their passionate pleas before me and others, and I highly regarded them as examples to follow.

Paul says to the Thessalonians to "pray without ceasing." This concept, of course, is not that you go around speaking prayers aloud all the time or drive with your eyes closed in moments of prayer. That is absurd! What Paul is suggesting is that believers should be in a constant attitude of prayer—that the communication line between them and God is wide open because no sin impedes their access to His throne.

I personally saw the miraculous way God answered the prayers of my family when doctors told us my mother would not live through Christmas

Eve night or that she would not survive without preventive treatment for cancer. The year after doctors told us she would die in six months without radiation or chemotherapy, my mother jogged on Atlantic Beach, celebrated God's healing, and did so for the next five years. I witnessed God's perfect plan through what I believe to have been the "effectual, fervent prayers" of my own and the church family.

Prayer is a continual communication with God, much as we converse with family members. It is a natural outcome of that interpersonal relationship.

To illustrate, I once heard a story about a young minister who had just arrived at his new ministry. For whatever reason, the young man was to stay with one of the elder saints of the church until the people could provide other accommodations. The young pastor was thrilled at the news because the older gentleman had a reputation of being a prayer warrior.

After the young man became comfortable with his surroundings, he decided to find the secret to the man's prayer vigilance. Since he had not observed any unusual prayer practices from the elder, he decided to camp just outside the gentleman's door after the elder retired to his bedroom. In this location, the young preacher expected to hear something like, "O thou who sitteth upon the realm of the universe . . ." resound from the room. He listened intently and heard the following instead: "Good night, Lord. See you in the morning." This saint walked so closely with the Lord that he conversed with God all day, every moment an attitude of prayer. That intimate, personal prayer life is what God desires for us all.

Beyond having an awe of God, studying His word, and praying together, what can we do to restore biblical values in ourselves, children, and others? What can we do so that we can cast that all-important shadow?

Brainstorming is key to generating thoughts in a writing endeavor, so why not try brainstorming to analyze the needs in our hearts, homes, and churches? For example, brainstorm what qualities you would like your children to develop, and make a list of ways you could teach or model those qualities. Ask yourself some tough questions about your shadows. For example, would I support my children if they said that serving on the mission field in Africa was their desire? Am I a hovering parent or friend who tries to dictate my child's or another's life? Do I allow my children or those under my influence to develop their own talents, or do I pressure them to follow my career choice? Do I regularly run interference between God and a friend or a child's difficulties? Do I admit to others when I am wrong? I believe you see the need for determining your own crucial questions.

Once the brainstorming is complete, analyze the list and questions to see if they line up with God's will expressed in Scripture. If so, then examine the biblical dictates that will produce those traits and values in your children. Seek to live out those dictates and commit your best to the Lord each day through a directed effort—the head-on-pillow promise or the wet-shirt work ethic.

Suppose a concern for the welfare of others was among that list of true values. Is that not what we hear so much in the media as the world's viewpoint? The Bible is just as clear; we need to meet the needs of others and our environment. Jesus, *others*, and you (JOY). Obviously, God does not oppose this focus. He commands us to esteem others better than ourselves. He expects us to be good stewards of all that He has given to us (1 Peter 4:10). When we do so, we work soup kitchens, we help our neighbors recoup after a storm, we visit the sick, etc. Though today we have turned JOY into *YOJ*, it is definitely never too late to turn the word around. I *encourage* you to invest in others.

What if we genuinely believed what we say we believe? For example, does hell really exist? If we honestly believe it does, and we believe that God does not desire for anyone to suffer there for all eternity, would we not be more earnest in lovingly sharing the gospel with others? Of course, our children should be our first concern, making sure they understand and have accepted the Lord as their Savior. Why do we not witness to others as well and allow our children to see our passion for the lost?

May I suggest that discomfort with confronting others about the condition of their souls has taken the place of a loving concern. If God commissioned the Holy Spirit to pursue the lost one, and if the Holy Spirit is alive in us, then He will guide us and will provide all we need to witness to that lost one. We can depend upon Him to provide the necessary words when the witnessing begins, especially if we are regularly in that Word and regularly committing it to memory.

Nothing thrills a Christian like seeing another soul come to Christ! Nothing would be a greater scene for our children to witness than seeing someone led to Christ. Or even better, imagine how wonderful it would be if our children were the instruments God used to bring someone to Himself. If you feel unsure about which Scriptures to use or what to say, just share what Christ has done personally for you. That, my friend, is a testimony. If you have not tried it, I *encourage* you to do so. You will be amazed at what God will do!

I *encourage* you to show biblical respect for those in authority, even if you view them as enemies. Matthew 5:43–44 (ESV) says, "You have heard that it was said, 'You shall love your neighbor and hate your enemy.' But I say to you, Love your enemies and pray for those who persecute you." As citizens of heaven, we have an obligation to submit to the authority over us upon earth and the authority of heaven. Jesus said, "Render to Caesar the things that are Caesar's and to God the things that are God's" (Mark 12:17). We have a duty to teach a respect for authority to those who follow. We show obedience to God's authority when we respect and even pray for our leaders and, yes, our enemies.

I personally have had conflicting views with authorities before and did not really know how to give respect I did not have. I sought the advice of my pastors on two separate occasions. The advice, however, was the same from both: pray for the success of that authority and respect the office of the authority if I could not respect the person.

My initial response was an emphatic, "What?! I am to pray for his success?" My pastor friend assured me that he meant exactly what he had said: I was to pray for the man who was giving me such grief. I must confess that my prayers for the success of that authority began much like this, "Lord, please make Mr. _____ successful! In Jesus's name, Amen!" After a few days the prayers became more like, "Dear Lord, I am praying on Mr. _____'s behalf that you will do a work in his life that will produce for him success physically, emotionally, and more importantly spiritually. In the precious name of Jesus, my Savior." Before long, my prayers were heartfelt pleas for that man's spiritual and earthly success. The man did not change; however, my attitude toward him was the change. Instead of privately badmouthing him, I learned to pray for him.

When another challenge with authority came my way, I approached my then pastor about the situation. He agreed with me when I said, "Let me guess how I am to solve this issue. Pray for the person's success?" I'm sure you know his answer.

The conflict needed greater resolution than I could provide, but my attitude toward that person changed. I truly prayed for their success and continued to worship at our church. I learned that the way to accept the authority over me was to pray for that person's needs instead of speaking out against that person. If we do not publicly rant and rave at others, perhaps those who follow us would not believe they had a right to rant and rave against authority.

I *encourage* you to love God with all your heart and with all your soul and with all your mind and with all your strength (Mark 12:30 ESV). Praise God, I have a legacy of family members who loved God. Yes, they, like me and you, were sinners saved by grace, and yes, their ways were not always perfect. However, I saw in them the desire to live the best they could, not through self-effort but through commitment to God's Word. I witnessed in them the light and salt of which the Bible speaks. All of them had their own way, their own personalities, and their own impacts upon me and others. In the greatest times of trial and tribulation, I saw the hope they had in God.

My forefathers and mothers lived through the Depression, wars, loss of children, loss of spouses, and loss of property, but I never saw them or knew them to experience loss of faith or hope. Their God was real, and my God is real. Their hope was in God because He is constant. He was the Light in their darkest hours, and they took comfort in His shadow. If you are still asking if it is ever too late to invest in your children or in those who follow you, the answer is another resounding response . . . no!

Let me reiterate the conclusion of the whole matter. You and I have a legacy to leave to the younger generations and to this present age. Their inheritance will be an understanding of what it means to know Christ as Savior and have that intimate, personal relationship with Him. Their inheritance is the truth of God's Word and the value of the Word, as Jesus Christ revealed His instructions for life before leaving this earth. Their inheritance is also an understanding that the effectual, fervent prayer of a righteous man or woman avails much (James 5:16).

I have a legacy to leave to this world: I am to point out the inexplicable workings of God that occur around me every day and to claim them as such before those who follow me. That legacy will show them a humble spirit and a confession of my struggles and failures so that they will see me not as self-righteous but just as I am and they are—a sinner saved by grace who messes up.

My legacy will show them that God is not only a loving God, but He is also a righteous, holy God. He does not laugh at sin but abhors it, and I will pay the consequences of that sin in my life and in eternity through the absence of reward. I have often heard it said, "You can choose the sin, but you can never choose the consequences. God does." That adage is absolutely and scripturally true! I have a God-given responsibility to shadow the truth of sin's consequences.

I have a legacy to leave to this world: to show forth the fruit of the Spirit so others can see that fruit in action. No one can take the fruit of the spirit from me. I only hide it with my own agendas, my own complaints, and my own sins.

My legacy displays a work ethic that says I will always seek to do my best to honor and glorify the Lord God. My legacy is an unconditional love for others but not always for what they do. What I wink at, I tolerate, so I must be careful not to wink too often or even at all.

My legacy is a life well lived before them, not in the accumulation of things but in the values and biblical principles I abide by. I heard it said recently, "What we do in moderation, our kids will do in excess." Even if I am able to live out the Word only moderately, perhaps my students will live Him excessively in the very right way. Maybe they will become "not just a fan, but a committed follower," as Kyle Idleman suggests in his book, *Not a Fan*.[4] That inheritance is an adoption into the family of God.

So, my friend, let me *encourage* you that it is never too late to apologize to your children, fellow workers, family members, and all people in your lives—to come clean about your failures before them. It is never too late to repent of the lifestyle that you have lived out that others have witnessed. It is never too late to confess that you have had your priorities out of sync. It is never too late to tell others you were wrong in railing against the authority of God or another person. It is never too late to show your love for your children by apologizing for not setting boundaries and lovingly disciplining. It is never too late to begin a proper legacy and give them a godly inheritance.

After all, God is our *hope*. He is the one to run to with our infirmities, our sins, our doubts, and our fears. He is the perfect model to aspire to be like. He understands we are flawed and just desires for us to surrender ourselves and the ones we love into His care. He is the faithful One. He is the Light of the world in whose shadow we are to stand. He is the inheritance we are to leave to our children.

The journalist I spoke of at this book's beginning was confident that an emerging young political star was out there. She recognized the need to nurture that young candidate so that he or she would be equipped to impact the future of this nation. While political aspirations are worthy goals, there is a far greater need to impact the world for the cause of Christ. God has always preserved a remnant—the body of believers—to proclaim His message. An emerging David is out there somewhere, ready to stand against the Goliath of the day. An emerging Esther is waiting for such a time as this. An emerging Paul is open to preaching the Word and ready to serve. We must be the nurturers and equip them for the future of the kingdom. We must shine the Light that casts the *solid* shadow.

Is it too late to invest in a legacy for future generations? The answer is undeniably no!

Acknowledgments

WITHOUT THE LORD JESUS CHRIST, I CAN DO NOTHING. I AM MOST grateful for His sustaining grace and power in my life through His salvation—the finished work of His death, burial, and resurrection. It is only through Him that I live. Thankfully, He bestowed upon me the godly heritage of which I write.

Though they are now with the Lord, with a grateful heart I thank my mother, father, maternal grandparents, and paternal grandparents for Christlike examples lived out before me. I am abundantly thankful for the prayerful support of family and friends who encouraged me to pursue what I struggled to believe was possible.

Among those friends and family are the ones who were gracious enough to read, edit, and offer suggestions for this writing. Thank you, Larry Doig, for your careful perusal and notes but most importantly for living out Christ to your children and your children's children; that life was a constant example for me as well. Much appreciation to you, Brenda, for being his steadfast companion and Christlike example.

Thank you, Mary Lou Shearer, Carolyn Thomas, and Pat Zirkle, for being dear, faithful friends and for giving me your insights for the book's progression. Thank you, Pat Stewart, for reminding me constantly that "God's got you!"

Thank you, Dr. Jay Knolls, for the extensive notes, suggestions, and encouragements throughout your reading of the book and for proclaiming the truth of Scripture.

Thank you, Teresa Sholy, for the beautiful front cover images, your thoughtful comments, and your steadfast friendship.

Thank you, Bob and Cathy Canterbury (now with the Lord), for being spiritual parents to me throughout my adult years.

Thank you, Jared Ball, for all your instruction to this technology-challenged writer.

Thank you, Lord, for guiding me to Redemption Press. I am grateful to B. J. Garrett; I knew from the moment you prayed that God is your constant guide and friend. Dori Harrell, you have been such an encouragement to me throughout the editing process. You, in your wisdom, gave me Hannah McKenzie as a delightful project manager and Lesley Ann McDaniel as editor and coach. Thank you, Lesley, for your patience, your professional advice, and your kinship. You made the revision coaching a joy. Seeing my friend Teresa's creativity come to fruition in the cover design is the work of Nate. Thank you. Carrie De Pizzo and Kim Silva are amazing editors; I appreciate you both so very much. Redemption Press's professionalism and timely responses have been a witness of its mission for God and His kingdom. I deeply appreciate all that you have done on my behalf.

Thank you that my project manager Hannah assigned the very capable Mari Gonzales as my new project manager as God has called Hannah to different role. Her kindness and understanding have been an encouragement.

Words are never enough to express the magnitude of appreciation to you all.

Notes

1. Harper Lee, *To Kill a Mockingbird* (New York, Grand Central Publishing, 1988).

2. Mary J. Cartwright, "The Old Ship of Zion" (Wikipedia Foundation, June 6, 2020).

3. "Greed," *Wikipedia*, Wikipedia Foundation, 9 June 2020, web.

4. Kyle Idlman, *Not a Fan* (Grand Rapids, MI: Zondervan, 2016).

ORDER INFORMATION

To order additional copies of this book, please visit
www.redemption-press.com.
Also available at Amazon, Christian bookstores,
and Barnes and Noble.

CPSIA information can be obtained
at www.ICGtesting.com
Printed in the USA
JSHW081755160323
39012JS00004B/23